STRENGTH &
FITNESS TRAINING

STRENGTH & FITNESS TRAINING

ALL YOU NEED TO KNOW ABOUT EXERCISING FOR STRENGTH AND FITNESS IN MORE THAN 300 EXPERT PHOTOGRAPHS

A STEP-BY-STEP GUIDE TO WORKING THE MUSCLES USING FREE WEIGHTS, BODY WEIGHT EXERCISES AND MACHINE WEIGHTS

ANDY WADSWORTH

southwater

This edition is published by Southwater,
an imprint of Anness Publishing Ltd,
Blaby Road, Wigston,
Leicestershire LE18 4SE; info@anness.com

www.southwaterbooks.com; www.annesspublishing.com

If you like the images in this book and would like to investigate using them
for publishing, promotions or advertising, please visit our website
www.practicalpictures.com for more information.

Publisher: Joanna Lorenz
Project Editor: Anne Hildyard
Designer: Nigel Partridge
Illustrator: Peter Bull
Production Controller: Bessie Bai

ETHICAL TRADING POLICY
At Anness Publishing we believe that business should be conducted
in an ethical and ecologically sustainable way, with respect for the
environment and a proper regard to the replacement of the natural
resources we employ. As a publisher, we use a lot of wood pulp to make
high-quality paper for printing, and that wood commonly comes from
spruce trees. We are therefore currently growing more than 750,000 trees
in three Scottish forest plantations: Berrymoss
(130 hectares/320 acres), West Touxhill (125 hectares/305 acres)
and Deveron Forest (75 hectares/185 acres). The forests we manage
contain more than 3.5 times the number of trees employed each year
in making paper for the books we manufacture. Because of this ongoing
ecological investment programme, you, as our customer, can have the
pleasure and reassurance of knowing that a tree is being cultivated on
your behalf to naturally replace the materials used to make the book
you are holding. Our forestry programme is run in accordance with the
UK Woodland Assurance Scheme (UKWAS) and will be certified by the
internationally recognized Forest Stewardship Council (FSC). The FSC is a
non-government organization dedicated to promoting responsible manage-
ment of the world's forests. Certification ensures forests are managed in
an environmentally sustainable and socially responsible way. For further
information about this scheme, go to www.annesspublishing.com/trees

Previously published as part of a larger volume, *The Complete Practical
Encyclopedia of Fitness Training*

CONTENTS

Introduction

If your aim is to build physical strength and improve your muscle tone, a properly supervised training plan will help you to achieve your goal. You could go to the gym and use variable resistance machines there, but it is also beneficial to introduce exercises that use your body weight in conjunction with free weights, so that if for any reason you cannot get to the gym, you will still be able to carry on with your usual exercise routine.

This book will give you an understanding of which exercises will help you to achieve your goals, with detailed descriptions of how and when to do them so that you can be confident that you are exercising correctly. To achieve fast, effective, long-lasting results you will need variation in your training. Each exercise lists the muscles used so you can determine which part of your body is being exercised, giving you the chance to change your exercises and challenge your body to promote better results.

As opposed to weight lifting, which makes bigger muscles and an increased body weight, strength training, combined with a calorie controlled diet and some form of cardiovascular exercise, builds muscle, but at the same time, it burns fat and does not increase body weight.

Before you begin exercising, decide what you want from your exercise routine. Do you want a six-pack for a summer beach holiday? Is building muscle or losing weight important for you? Whichever it is, there is a plan for achieving your goal in this book.

It's not just exercise that will make you fit and healthy; nutrition is just as important. Everything you eat has some effect on you – your food can turn to fat or energize you; it can help you to improve your fitness level, recover from exercise, change your body shape and alter your self-image. This book will provide you with an understanding of the effect that different foods have, the optimum nutrition combination and the best time to eat and drink.

There is always some exercise you can do. Even if you are injured, there are exercises that will help you to recover. This book provides you with basic knowledge to help with diagnosing injury, understanding the recovery process and preventing the injury from recurring.

Exercise is not just about sweating buckets in the gym. Core stability and flexibility training are just as important to prevent injury and give you the strength to train harder, push big weights, run marathons or cope with the demands of everyday life.

Regular exercising will not only help you to gain physical fitness, providing a big boost to your self-esteem; you will also have increased energy, and benefit from a more active and positive outlook.

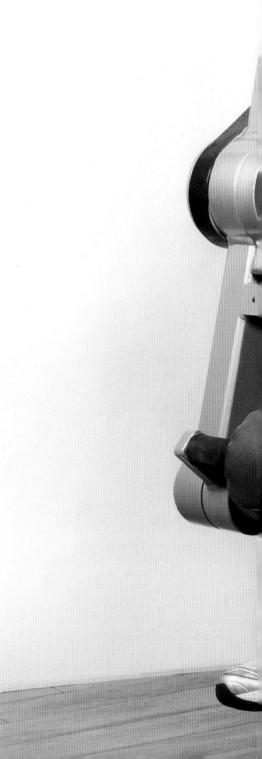

Right: Building physical strength is much easier if you have a controlled and supervised training plan.

GETTING STARTED

Before you begin your journey to a fitter lifestyle, this chapter outlines a realistic approach to a successful fitness training programme, including accurately assessing your starting point, setting achievable goals, performing fitness tests to measure your progress, and determining which exercises are best for you. You will come to appreciate why you are not intended to live a sedentary lifestyle, and commit to making health and exercise priorities in your life.

Above: Dumbbells are used to develop the pectoral muscles.
Left: Dips are exercises that work the muscles surrounding the chest.

Training Diary

Keeping a training diary will help you to achieve your goals and stay motivated. Make the diary realistic and useful. Don't cram it with information that will become irrelevant later on in training – only note facts that motivate you and help you to track your progress.

A diary can help to re-motivate you as you look back through all the other fitness improvements you have made.

When losing weight you may find that over the first six weeks of training you lose 10kg/22lb but then you don't lose any in the seventh week, which can lessen your motivation. However, it's not just the weight loss that matters; for example, if you have been walking in an effort to accelerate your weight loss, and could only walk for 1.6km/1 mile in your first week, but can now manage 4.8km/3 miles, this progress will motivate you to keep going.

If you are training for a marathon, keep a diary of all your training, including details such as whether your training is road or off-road running, the time of day, your nutrition and hours of sleep. This way, if you do suffer from any problems, such as an overuse injury, a coach or physician will be able to use your diary to see when the problems may have started and may be able to determine what caused them. Noting what you eat will help you determine which foods work best for your performance and recovery.

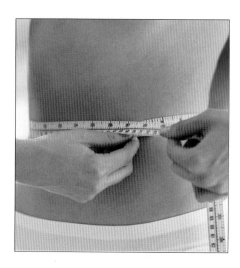

Above: By taking your measurements, you can work out that you have lost fat and are more toned than before.

Above: If you step up your walking, note the details in your diary, to allow you to assess your progress better.

How to keep your training diary
You should record details of your training, the goals you want to achieve and an assessment of your training to date. Include test results, nutrition information and body measurements.
Daily records Record the following information in your diary every day:
• The physical training you intend to do against the actual physical training that took place, marked out of ten.
• Hours of sleep the previous night.
• Resting heart rate, taken first thing in the morning.
• Any injury or signs of fatigue.
• All food and fluid intake, including what time you ate or drank.

Also note what you did on rest days, as your activity on these days will have a significant effect on your performance. For example, if you stayed up late on a rest day, or drank alcohol on two rest days before a big competition, your performance will suffer and when you check the diary you will know why.

Above: Your training needs to work the way you want it to. You can discuss your progress with an instructor at the gym.

Big goals and small goals At the front of your diary list the goals you want to achieve, and when you want to achieve them by. For example, if you weigh 70kg/154lb on 1 January and you want to lose 10.8kg/24lb over six months, or 1.8kg/4lb per month, mark your desired weight – your small goal – on the appropriate page for each month; so on the page for 1 February, you would note that you want to weigh 68kg/150lb, and on the page for 1 March, you would note that you want to weigh 66kg/146lb, and so on.
Weekly assessment At the end of each week assess how your training has gone. Note the average score you have given to your training and how you felt each day. Look back over your nutrition for the week and mark down any changes you want to make. Assess your fluid intake for the week and check that you are drinking enough. Add up the total number of hours you have been

Below left: Note any injury; what you were doing and for how long. It may help you alter your training plan.

Below middle: An accurately filled-in training diary can prove to be an invaluable asset at a later date.

Below right: Keep a record of the hours that you sleep to get an insight into your sleeping patterns.

training and compare it with the week before. Make a note of measurements such as body fat, weight and Body Mass Index (BMI).

Weekly review If the overview of your week is not positive, consider where you may have gone wrong and note the changes that you intend to make in order to get more from your training. These changes might involve a different combination of exercises, taking more

Above: Even if your goal seems daunting at times, try to meet the challenge and stay on track.

rest days or working harder to achieve intensity levels in certain sessions. Look back at the goals you have set yourself, written at the front of the diary, and make changes to the small goals – adding new ones and ticking off the ones that you have achieved.

Body Type

We are all born with a body type, some naturally physically stronger than others. However, with the right exercise and nutrition, we can become stronger and fitter, change our type and fine-tune our strengths for specific sports and physical activities.

Your body type will have a direct influence on your sporting performance. For example, if you are a gymnast or Tour de France cyclist, being lightweight is a priority. However, if you take part in contact sports or weightlifting, you need to be heavy enough to hold your ground in the scrum or have the muscle power and strength to lift weights.

American psychologist W.H. Sheldon (1898–1977) developed a system in the 1940s that recognized three body types: endomorph, mesomorph and ectomorph. Most people share many, but not all, of the features of one of these body types.

Endomorphs
People with this body shape carry the most body mass of all three types. They are pear-shaped and often overweight. Endomorphs are likely to have the most sedentary lifestyles of all of the body types. They are not good at endurance activities, but if they have strong enough muscles, they can lift weights and use their own weight to provide power. Consequently, disciplines such as javelin and hammer throwing naturally suit them. People of this body type have a high Body Mass Index (BMI) and are at a greater risk of poor health than any other body type.

Mesomorphs
The most athletic and muscular-looking of the three body types, mesomorphs find it easy to compete in most sports and are able to build lean muscle, lose and gain weight fast, and maintain low body fat. They are stronger and fitter than other body types and will be good at adapting their body to cardiovascular and strength-training exercises. Mesomorphs are at less risk of health problems than any other body type. Mesomorphs can train harder than any other body type but need to watch their diet to make sure they are getting the correct fuel for their activity; they can get away with eating unhealthy food much of the time, but it won't provide them with the fuel for activity or aid their recovery after exercise.

Ectomorphs
These are the most fragile of the body types. They are thin in appearance and struggle to gain weight. Their low level of body fat makes them more susceptible to health problems. However, they are the best body type for endurance activities such as running marathons or cycling long distances. With the correct training, ectomorphs can have very high power-to-weight ratios, making them fast over long distances and good at climbing hills, for example.

Left: Some people are more flexible than others, but this degree of flexibility requires more than just genetics.

Above: Try a regime to change your body shape and, as a result, you will be happier with the way you look.

Making the changes
You may be an endomorph now but this doesn't mean you have to stay that way. The right exercise and food will change your body shape and decrease the risk of health problems. If you want to have a more athletic figure, you will need to follow a plan that involves burning as many calories as possible, while eating healthily, using the glycaemic index as a guideline in order to balance your blood sugar levels and prevent you from depositing fat. You will need to exercise three to four times a week,

A combined approach
To change your body type, you will need to adjust your training and your nutrition. One without the other will never get you the desired result. Once you have changed the way you look, you will need to continue working hard to maintain your new body shape.

Above: Ectomorphs are naturally thin and have a low level of body fat. They often find it hard to gain weight.

Above: Mesomorphs are the fittest, with more lean muscle and low body fat. They easily lose and gain weight.

Above: Endomorphs have the largest body mass and may be overweight. They often have a sedentary lifestyle.

incorporating: cardiovascular training to burn calories and build a better and more efficient aerobic system (which in turn will allow you to burn yet more calories); and resistance training to build muscle and increase your metabolism.

Left: If you eat a healthy diet and exercise appropriately, you will be able to alter your body image.

Endomorph to mesomorph If you are an endomorph, the chances are that you constantly struggle to motivate yourself to eat healthily and exercise. To make the necessary changes, you will need to alter your habits. Focus on reducing your calorie intake and increasing cardiovascular fitness and resistance training to increase your metabolism and lose weight. As you feel the benefits and increase your energy levels, you should see results more quickly, which will, in turn, reinforce your motivation.

Ectomorph to mesomorph You will need to consume more calories to feed your muscles and help them grow. At the same time you need to reduce your cardiovascular training time and focus more on resistance training, which will help you to build muscle.

Mesomorph to endomorph This is the easiest transformation and one that, unfortunately, usually happens quite by

accident. People who were athletic in their youth but have less time for exercise as they grow older, and perhaps have a sedentary job, are likely to change body type in this way. The bottom line is that if you consume more calories than you expend, then an endomorph you will become.

Mesomorph to ectomorph If you have bulky muscles, you may want to change shape, but this is hard to do. It requires you to lose muscle, not just fat. You can try to lose muscle by reducing your calorie intake so that you have to burn up muscle and use it as an energy source. Add long-distance endurance running or cycling, but avoid resistance training, as this will build muscle.

Altering your body type
Expect changes to your body shape to take time. Don't be discouraged by this. Keep the end goal in sight and stay motivated. If your body type changes too quickly, you will not be able to sustain the transformation.

Strength Tests

When devising a training plan – and before you actually embark on it – it is important to find out how strong you are. Otherwise, you could quickly overreach yourself and do yourself an injury. When measuring your strength, use a test that best suits you and your specific goals.

The test that you choose should be determined by the goal you have in mind. If you want bigger arms, then use bicep and tricep exercises to generate a test that will assess your performance on the way to achieving your goals.

To recover from a knee operation using exercise to build strength in your quadriceps, use a leg extension test to assess the strength in your quadriceps and monitor your rehabilitation programme.

If you want stronger, wider shoulders, do shoulder presses in order to assess shoulder strength.

Below: Test your body for strength on the areas that you most want to work out.

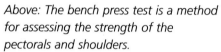

Above: The bench press test is a method for assessing the strength of the pectorals and shoulders.

To assess hamstring strength (muscles at the back of the thigh), use a hamstring curl machine.

For upper-back strength, do chin-ups and add weights, wearing a weights belt to test your strength.

Take precautions
Before you do any strength test for the first time, consult your doctor. If you are testing to find your one repetition maximum (ORM), make sure to have a training partner to help you when your muscles tire. Use supports and foot rests on exercise machines when you start to fail on a weight. Struggling to lift a weight that is too heavy for you is one of the most common causes of injuries.

Above: You can easily find out how strong your legs are by using the leg press.

One Repetition Maximum test
This is the gold standard of strength tests. Most ORM tests involve the bench press and leg press, as these two exercises involve the majority of the large muscles in the upper and lower body. Follow this procedure to find your ORM:
1 Warm up for three sets using a weight you can lift for at least ten repetitions.
2 Add 5–10 per cent to the weight and complete three repetitions.
3 Add a further 5–10 per cent to the weight and try to complete three repetitions.
4 Continue to add 5–10 per cent to the weight until you can only do one repetition (ORM).

Strength assessment					
Bench press	**Poor**	**Fair**	**Good**	**Very good**	**Excellent**
Male	0.6	0.8	1.0	1.2	1.4
Female	0.3	0.4	0.5	0.6	0.7
Leg press					
Male	1.4	1.8	2.0	2.4	2.8
Female	1.2	1.4	1.8	2.0	2.2

Left: The sit-up test lifts the head and shoulders up. It measures the strength of the abdominal muscles and hip flexor muscles. The more sit-ups you can do in 1 minute, the stronger your muscles.

Once you have found your ORM for the bench press and leg press, divide the weight you have achieved by your body weight to get a score. This is the calculation if your ORM for the bench press is 100kg/220lb:

100kg/220lb (ORM bench press)/ 80kg/176lb (body weight) = 1.25

A good result for a male would be more than 1.4; a poor result is less than 0.6.

Strength endurance test
You can easily do this test at home. It involves doing as many sit-ups and press-ups as possible in 1 minute. Because women do not have the same upper-body strength as men, women can do the press-ups with their knees on the floor. Use the scores in the table to assess your strength endurance.

Using the strength tests
Anyone can adapt the strength tests to their chosen sport. For example, if you are a cyclist, use the leg press to find your ORM. For the strength endurance test, see how many step-ups or squats you can do in 1 minute. If you want to build a bigger, stronger chest, do an ORM test using the bench press, and for strength endurance, do as many press-ups as you can manage in 1 minute. Repeat every four to six weeks to monitor your progress.

Right: For the female press-up test, the knees balance on the floor.

Above right: The male technique for a press-up test lifts the body off the floor.

Strength endurance assessment					
Sit-ups	Poor	Fair	Good	Very good	Excellent
Male	20	30	40	50	60
Female	10	20	30	40	50
Press-ups					
Male	10	20	30	40	50
Female	10	20	30	40	50

Equipment for Strength Training

With both free weights and machines, expensive equipment, though preferable, is by no means necessary. It is much more important that you combine different pieces of equipment for maximum effect – and know how to use them correctly and safely.

You don't need to spend lots of money on strength-training equipment, but if money is no obstacle, then having expensive, well-built equipment may well help to motivate you to exercise. This equipment is normally the easiest to adjust to suit your personal needs; it will offer a greater range of movements and require less maintenance.

You can choose between using free weights, body weight or machine weights, such as weight-training benches, squat stands, single stations and multi-gyms. Or, you can use a combination of all three for the best workouts. No single piece of equipment is better than any other piece. The most important factor is how you use the equipment. If used correctly, you will benefit from it; if used incorrectly, you may do yourself more harm than good.

Below: In a gym, dumbbells are stored on a convenient rack according to their size.

Use of free weights

Free weights such as dumbbells or barbells require you to recruit more muscle mass to provide balance and stability, unlike machines, which simply require you to push a weight in one direction. Free weights demand that you control the weight in all directions.

Free weights

Free weights involve barbells or dumbbells.
Barbells These are long, straight bars with weight plates attached at each end. Some gyms have a variety of barbells, with the plates permanently fixed to the bar. Sometimes, the plates can be removed so that you can adjust the barbell size and weight. If you intend using adjustable barbells, make sure that you use the safety collars on each end to retain the weights.
Dumbbells These are short bars with weighted plates on each end. The plates

may be fixed or removable, depending on the size of the weights area. Most gyms have a variety of dumbbells with permanently fixed plates.

If you want to use equipment at home, free weights are a good option compared with machines. Machines take up a lot of room and may give you the option of working only one or two different exercises – unless you've bought a multi-gym (a unit with lots of exercise stations coming off it). By contrast, free weights take up very little room and can be used for a variety of exercises.

Weight machines

Machines with multiple weight stacks give you an easily adjustable weight. You simply adjust the weights stack with a connecting pin that runs through the middle of the weight you want to select.

Below: This weights bench is adjustable to most sizes but it is best to check first that it is suitable for you.

Above: Before exercising, adjust the machine to fit you correctly. If it does not feel comfortable, do not use it.

Machines are often seen as safer because you cannot drop the weights on the floor or lose your balance, or even control of the weight, and injure yourself. Be warned: machines can sometimes be designed in such a way that they do not 'fit' you very well. Setting up machines in the correct position for you takes experience and, possibly, some assistance from a qualified instructor. You could unknowingly put yourself in a position that will cause muscle or joint pain. For example, sitting on a chest-press machine with the handles set too high will force your shoulders to do all of the work, not your chest. Some machines are designed as 'one size fits all', but they do not always live up to their billing. If you are particularly short or tall, you need to ask yourself whether a

---

Start right

Make sure the machines you use are set up correctly, with the back, seat and any handles or levers involved in the correct position. Once you are actually pushing or pulling the weight, there should be no strain on any part of your body; it should feel comfortable and natural.

---

particular machine is going to be best for you. How can you tell? Quite simply, if it feels wrong or awkward when you try to use it, use free weights instead.

Make sure that you are completely familiar with the safety aspects of each machine that you will be using before you start training on it. For example, if you are going to use a leg-press machine, before you release the weight and start bending your legs back toward your body, be clear about what you need to do in case you fatigue and you cannot straighten your legs again. Always check to see whether there is any kind of safety mechanism to stop your legs being crushed.

Body weight

If you are in a restricted space, or have a limited budget, then simply use your body weight – it's highly effective. Even top bodybuilders use exercises such a press-ups and lunges. To make these exercises effective, make sure that you are using the correct technique to isolate the muscles you want to work and avoid injury. Using just your body weight in warm-up exercises is also a great way to stimulate the muscles you intend to work using free weights or machines, giving you a better workout all round.

Getting started

If you do join a gym, you are most likely to be shown how to use the machines for your strength training. But if you find

---

Use a mirror

Where possible, when exercising, you will need to use a full-length mirror, especially when doing free weights and body-weight exercises. Looking into the mirror will enable you to check your technique, and confirm that you are working the correct muscles. Use a mirror to adjust your training procedures.

---

you are mainly using machines in your workouts, take time to vary your exercise and introduce exercises that involve just your body weight and free weights. That way, you always have a familiar exercise programme when you are staying away from home and have limited or no access to a gym.

For weight-training, wear comfortable clothing that allows you the full range of movement. Clothing that fits close to your skin will enable you to see if the correct muscles are working. Always wear a number of layers to make it easy to adjust to changes in the temperature you are working in, and to keep your muscles warm.

Below: You can easily assess your position and ensure good technique by looking in a full-length mirror.

RESISTANCE TRAINING: LOWER BODY

Using resistance training techniques can tone and shape the legs, as well as strengthen them. This chapter outlines the numerous muscles in the lower body, and how to work them effectively. The exercises include simple squats and presses for beginners, general leg exercises, and training for specific muscles in the upper and lower legs, such as the quadriceps, hamstrings, thigh muscles and calf muscles.

Above: A machine leg curl is a good way to stretch out the hamstrings.
Left: A cable single-leg extension works the quadriceps, the large muscles in the thighs.

Benefits and Principles of Resistance Training

After the age of 30, your metabolic rate starts to decrease every year. Resistance training involves applying resistance to a movement that will not only increase your metabolic rate, but also give you greater strength and more energy.

Resistance training will build muscle and can even reverse the inevitable decline in your metabolic rate. The afterburn (calories expended after exercise) of resistance training will burn far more calories than the afterburn of a cardiovascular session. Knowing that you are still burning calories when you are sitting at your desk, several hours after your training session, is a real bonus.

Resistance training and health

You can build and tone over 600 of your muscles using resistance training; it will help reduce the risk of injury, especially lower back injury, by promoting good balance, co-ordination and posture.

Sports that involve contact, such as rugby or American football, will take their toll on your body. The correct resistance training, however, will give you the strength you need to withstand the impact of the tackle or of falling to the ground. Endurance sports such as running require your muscles to

Below: Press-ups are one of the oldest resistance exercises, but they are still just as effective as ever.

Above: For any sports involving impact, such as American football, resistance training is essential to build muscle.

contract over and over again for long periods of time; resistance training will help give your muscles the strength they need to prevent overuse injuries. Changing your body shape through resistance training will give you improved self-esteem and will motivate you to keep up your training. There are also medical benefits to resistance

training. It will strengthen your bones and reduce the risk of bone degenerating disease such as osteoporosis. Resistance training will also help to lower your blood pressure, lower your resting heart rate, decrease the risk of diabetes, decrease the chance of certain cancers and promote an increase in high-density lipid (HDL) cholesterol, or good cholesterol.

Technique

Start by only using weights that are up to 75 per cent of your One Repetition Maximum (ORM). Each set should consist of at least 12 repetitions and at the end of each set you should feel as if you could do two more repetitions. Do no more than three sets of each exercise to avoid overtraining a muscle

Increase metabolic rate

Having muscle means having more living tissue that is available to burn calories; just in the same way a car with a big engine will burn more fuel than a car with a small engine.

Above: Get your trainer or training partner to check your technique while you are exercising.

group. To avoid muscle imbalances and promote good co-ordination, rotate your routine so that you use all your body parts in the week's training. Do not move on to other resistance training methods until you have completed six weeks of basic weight-training. Try to find a training plan that fits in with your goals.

Supersets These will help you to increase the intensity of your workout by decreasing the rest between exercises. This technique involves two exercises with just 5 seconds' rest between each exercise, followed by a 60–90 second rest at the end of a set before repeating.

Exercise opposing muscle groups, such as chest and back, hamstrings and quadriceps or triceps and biceps. This type of supersetting is great if you want to have an express workout or want to maintain a high heart rate to get cardiovascular benefits and to lose weight.

Pre-exhaustion supersets You may find that when you are working muscles in your upper body, your smaller muscles fatigue before you have worked the bigger muscles; for example, your triceps fatigue before you can work your pectorals hard enough. To combat this employ pre-exhaustion supersets using minimal rest. For example, to work the pectorals superset cable flies and bench presses. Only allow 5 seconds between each exercise so that the pectorals don't get a chance to recover.

Cheating repetitions Lift a weight to failure and then 'cheat' for a further two to three reps. For example, do a set of bicep curls to the point where you can't do another rep using the correct form and then try to do a further cheating rep swinging your upper body to help curl the weights up.

Forced repetitions Lift a weight to failure and then get your training partner to help you force out another two to three repetitions by adding just enough force to help you lift the weight.

Descending sets Lift a weight to failure and then quickly lower the weight so that you can continue with the set. Using a training partner to do this type of training is best, as it will reduce the time taken to decrease the weight during sets.

Burns Lift a weight to failure using full range of movement and correct technique, then do two to three further repetitions using a shorter range of movement.

Negative repetitions Resist the weight in the negative phase of movement, for example, loading the bench press with 100kg/220lb when your ORM is only 80kg/176lb and then resisting the bar as it lowers down to your chest. You may require a training partner to do this, as you will be using a weight that is greater than your ORM. If you don't have a training partner use safety catches to prevent injury.

Below: Cable machines are a very versatile training aid.

The Muscular System

Many people want to increase their muscle size. However, before you can even begin to think about effective training to achieve that goal, you need to understand how each of your muscles works to enable you to isolate the muscles you want to use.

Muscles are made up of bundles of fibres which are held in place by protective sheaths called fascia. The fibres are then subdivided into myofibrils. They contract when chemically stimulated by the nervous system and extend when the stimulation stops. Weight-training makes muscles grow by increasing the size of the myofibrils, which in turn increases the volume of blood flow to the muscle, the number of nerves that stimulate the muscle and the amount of connective tissue within the muscle cells. Myofibrils are divided again into bundles of myofilaments which are made up from chains of sarcomeres. As you reach the point of fatigue during resistance training, you will get small tears (microtears) in the myofilaments.

Below: The leaner you are, the easier it is to see the muscles you are working during resistance exercise.

During recovery after exercise your body will repair these small tears by giving the fibres nutrients which will also make these small fibres grow in size. The more exercise you do and the harder the intensity becomes, other

adaptations occur in the muscles. Muscles are able to store more glycogen which will enable the muscles to work even harder in the next workout. This also helps the muscles to slightly increase in size. As you lift a weight and

The muscles of the body

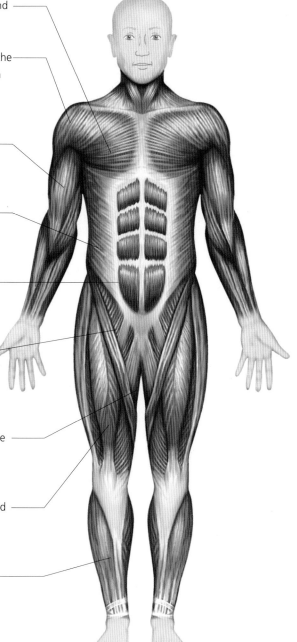

Pectorals these are used to push and pull the arms across the body.

Deltoids these are used to control the movement of the arms, taking them above the head, out to the side, in front and behind.

Biceps these are used to bend the arms at the elbow to bring the hands up toward you.

Obliques these are used to bend to the side and to control the twisting of the upper body.

Rectus abdominis these are used to bend the top half of the body forward.

Hip flexors these are used to lift the upper legs forward and upward.

Adductors these are used to pull the legs inward, toward the body.

Quadriceps these are used to extend and straighten the upper legs.

Tibialis anterior these are used to pull your feet upward, toward your shins.

Visualization
Think about what is going on inside your muscles to help you focus on keeping perfect technique throughout your training session.

cause tension in a muscle, more blood is transferred to that muscle, giving the muscle more oxygen and nutrients to provide energy for hard work.

The muscular nervous system
As you lift a weight and put your muscles under tension your nervous system sends a signal to the sheaths protecting the muscle fibres. This results in the muscle fibres contracting and the weight being lifted. It is important to use good technique in all your resistance training from the start, otherwise your

nervous system will adopt an incorrect sequence of movement, which long-term could lead to you sustaining an injury – and you won't get the desired results from your training. However, if your training is done correctly your nervous system will become even more efficient at telling your muscles when to work. Muscle recruitment is the key to getting stronger.

Right: The more toned you are, the more motivated you will feel about your workouts.

The muscles of the body

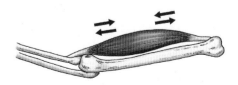

Neck muscles (semispinalis capitis muscle) these are used to move the head in a semi-circle from side to side, forward and backward.

Trapezius these are used to lift the shoulders upward and backward.

Rhomboids these are used for pulling movements; they help protect the spine.

Triceps these are used to push and to fully extend the arms.

Latissimus dorsi these are used to pull the arms into the body when there is resistance.

Abductors these are used to pull the legs outward, away from the body.

Gluteus maximus provide strength in powerful movements that involve most of the body. They maintain a connection between the legs and upper body.

Biceps femoris (hamstrings) these are used to bend the legs at the knees and lift them behind.

Gastrocnemius these are used to extend the feet when the legs are straight.

Soleus these are used to extend the feet when the legs are bent at the knee.

Muscular contractions

There are three types of muscular contractions:

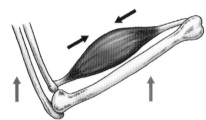

Concentric contraction
The arrows show a decrease in joint angle and muscle shortening. An example of this would be shortening your bicep muscle to bring your hand up toward you.

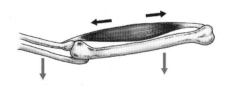

Eccentric contraction
The arrows show an increase in joint angle and muscle lengthening. An example of this would be lengthening of your bicep muscle as it lowers under resistance.

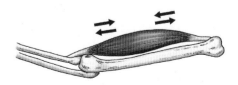

Isometric contraction
The arrows show no change in joint angle and muscle length under constant tension. An example of this would be tensing the abdominal muscles to stay in a fixed plank position.

Muscle Types

Now you know what the muscles of the body are called and where to find them. However, before you head straight to the gym, it is also important that you know what type of muscle you need to help you to achieve your goals.

Your body is made up of more than 250 million muscle fibres. Some muscle fibres consist of a high number of motor units per muscle fibre, such as muscles in the eye, which control small, precise movements. Other muscles, such as the quadriceps, need fewer motor units per muscle fibre, as they control bigger movements.

There are essentially two types of muscle fibre: Type I and Type II. Your genetic make-up does, to some extent, determine your muscle fibre type, but with the correct training and nutrition, you can change the percentage of each type. For endurance sports such as running and cycling, resistance training will give the muscles the strength they need.

Type I

These are also known as slow-twitch muscle fibres. They are red in colour as a result of their high myoglobin (a protein

Below: Long-distance marathon runners require Type I muscle fibres so they can sustain an effort for a long time.

Above: Cyclists who ride for long distances need Type I muscle fibres so they can keep going for long periods.

found in heart and skeletal muscles) content and have a high concentration of mitochondria (the 'power plant' of our cells, which use oxygen fat and sugar to release stored energy). A person with this type of muscle fibre is best at long-distance events such as Ironman triathlons or cross-country skiing. People with slow-twitch muscle fibre are likely to be smaller and have an ability to keep going for long periods of time. Type I muscle fibres contract more slowly than Type II muscle fibres, so people with this type of muscle are less good at movements such as throwing a ball fast or throwing a hard, fast punch.

Type II

These are also known as fast-twitch muscle fibres. They are white in colour due to a low myoglobin content and have a low concentration of mitochondria. People with this type

Which type of muscle fibre does your sport require?
This table shows the ratio of Type I muscle fibres to Type II muscle fibres that different athletes are likely to have, and also their VO2 max (ml/kg/min) as an indicator of the level of aerobic capacity they are likely to need for their sport.

Type of activity	Ratio of Type I to Type II	VO2 max ml/kg/min
Cyclist	60–40	60–75
Swimmer	55–45	55–65
Elite distance runner	80–20	70–80
American footballer	40–60	45–55
Ice hockey player	40–60	50–60
Cross-country skier	85–15	75–85
Rower	75–25	50–65
Sprinter	35–65	50–60

Above: Track cyclists need a higher percentage of Type II muscle fibres to pedal faster for short distances.

of muscle fibre are good at shorter athletic events because the muscle fibres contract faster. Power lifters and sprinters need a greater percentage of this type of muscle fibre. People with Type II muscle fibre appear bigger and have a larger amount of muscle mass. Type II muscle fibres can be split further into two subdivisions: IIa and IIb.

Type IIa is similar to a Type I muscle fibre in that it has adapted from being a Type II fibre to be able to assist in endurance events, such as cross-country skiing and marathon running. It is still able to contract fast but also has a well-developed capacity for both aerobic (the body's use of oxygen to generate energy) and anaerobic (without oxygen) energy transfer. This fibre type is more dependent than the others on a ready supply of oxygen.

Type IIb has the ability to work totally anaerobically, or without oxygen, and this athlete is capable of fast contractions using only anaerobic energy transfer.

Training the muscle types
It is possible to train muscle fibre to be of better use to you. For example, if you are a marathon runner, the more long-distance running you do, the better trained your Type I muscle fibre becomes. It is harder to train Type II muscle fibre.

Experiment with low-repetition weight-training on or close to your personal best, or sprint training with short recoveries.

One of the most effective ways of recruiting the fast-twitch muscle fibres is plyometrics training, because it activates the stretch-reflex mechanism of the muscle with an eccentric contraction. Plyometrics uses the acceleration and deceleration of body weight and includes exercises such as jumping and bouncing to enhance neuromuscular co-ordination of muscular movement.

In some sports it is hard to set training plans. For example, tennis requires lots of aerobic training to produce slow-twitch muscle fibres to give the player the endurance to last the entire match. However, this

steady cardiovascular training can interfere with the demand for high power output (fast-twitch muscle fibres) in the actual tennis strokes. Boxing is the same – being able to move around the ring constantly requires lots of endurance training and use of slow-twitch muscle fibres but the ability to give powerful punches means training your fast-twitch muscle fibres.

You should plan out your training sessions carefully, always being clear in your mind which type of muscle you want to train in each session.

Below: Sprinters require a higher percentage of Type II muscle fibres, which contract faster.

Resistance Training Safety

Every weight room in every gym should have on display a set of rules and regulations pertaining to safety. Make sure that you are fully aware of these rules and don't deviate from them. If you can't see one, ask a member of staff to point you in the right direction.

It is important that you always use the correct technique in all of your workout sessions. Do not copy the bad habits of other gym users who may be taking short cuts to make the training easier. Poor technique is a waste of time and effort because you will not be exercising the right muscles. Good technique, on the other hand, will help to prevent injuries, enabling you to train regularly and achieve your goals sooner. Use lighter weights than you think you might be capable of to start with in order to get your muscles used to the correct movements. Always make sure that you breathe in the correct way; holding your breath during a repetition will cause your blood pressure to rise and, in extreme cases, you could even pass out.

Training partner

If possible, train with another person. Your training partner can monitor and comment on your technique, and help you with heavier weights. If your partner is going to spot for you, make sure that you are both aware of what signal you will give when you are struggling. Your training partner will also need to know where to stand if he is going to spot for you. For example, in a seated dumbbell shoulder press, he needs to stand behind you and give support to your elbows to help you press the dumbbells up when you are struggling. In an Olympic bar bench press, your partner should stand behind your head, with both hands moving up and down close to the bar, ready to take the bar at any moment; or to help with the press when you start to struggle on the last few repetitions.

Equipment

Wear the correct clothing so that your body temperature does not go down after the warm-up. Have all the equipment you will need for the next few sets ready so that you are not waiting to go from one piece of equipment to the other. This way, you will stay in the right training zone, physically and mentally. Be safe when you are using the equipment – always use collars on the end of barbells and make sure racks have safety catches if you are training on your own. Put the equipment away after you have used it to avoid people tripping up – dumbbells rolling around on the floor are a safety hazard, and safety catches not fully engaged may cause severe injury. Always look to see what condition the equipment is in. Common problems include: dumbbells not screwed together correctly; bench press safety stoppers missing or not aligned correctly; loose foot supports; fraying cables; broken or loose seat supports; loose cable attachments; and slippery floors.

Warm-up

During resistance training, most injuries are caused by an inadequate warm-up and by attempting to lift weights that are too heavy. Warming up lubricates the tissues between the joints and

Below: Your trainer or training partner can check your position to ensure that you are exercising safely.

Above: Using a rowing machine is a good way to prepare your body before doing resistance training.

Warm-up procedure

Start with a light aerobic exercise such as jogging, cycling or rowing, depending on the body parts that you intend to use in the session. For example, do rowing if you are going to do a heavy session on the back muscles, or cycling if you are going to do a leg weights session.

Exercise for 5 minutes, then build the intensity for a further 5 minutes until your heart rate is up and you start to sweat and you begin to feel slightly short of breath.

For the next stage of the warm-up, simulate the movements you are going to be doing in the workout. For example, do three sets of ten squats if you are planning a leg exercising session, or three sets of ten shoulder presses with no weights if you are planning a shoulder workout.

Follow these exercises with some light stretches on the muscles you want to use, for example a quadriceps stretch for a leg workout and a cross-body shoulder stretch for a shoulder session. Hold each for 30 seconds at a time.

To finish the warm-up, use light weights and high repetitions on the first exercise that you want to do. Do one set of at least 20 repetitions before you move on to heavy weights.

increases the oxygenated blood supply to the muscles you want to work. It is essential to warm up correctly in order to prepare your muscles and joints for action in your exercise session. Wear a

number of layers in the gym to help maintain your body's temperature after the warm-up. You may need three to four layers in cold gyms or winter months. A good warm-up is an indispensable part of your routine for safe training and should never be skipped – even if it means that you have to cut your weight-lifting exercises short.

Below: Shoulder press movements are a good way to warm up the upper body before training.

Below: To prepare for a session in which you will use your legs, stretch the quadriceps beforehand.

Below: Stretch the shoulders to warm up the upper body in preparation for resistance training.

Leg Exercises for Beginners

There are more than 200 muscles in the lower half of the body, so it is no surprise that there are a great number of different leg exercises. To build up your leg muscles safely and effectively, start with these beginners' exercises.

Your legs are five times stronger than your arms because they have to support the body. To get real results from training your legs, you must be prepared to work hard. Take 2 to 3 seconds for each movement. Breathe in at the start of the movement and out as you return to the start position.

Static squat

Muscles used Quadriceps – rectus femoris, vastus lateralis, vastus intermedius

Squat with your back flat against the wall, feet in front of you, knees directly above your ankles, and thighs parallel to the floor. Hold for 60 seconds. When 60 seconds gets easy, make it harder by holding dumbbells.

Beginners' leg exercises	
Exercise	**Sets and repetitions**
Leg press	5 x 8–12
Dumbbell squat	5 x 8–12
Static squat	5 x 20-second holds

Dumbbell squat

Muscles used Quadriceps – rectus femoris, vastus lateralis, vastus intermedius; gluteus medius and maximus

1 *Stand with your feet shoulder-width apart. Hold a dumbbell in each hand, with your palms facing inward.*

2 *Bend your knees until your thighs are almost parallel to the floor. Pause for a second, then push back up.*

Barbell front squat

Muscles used Quadriceps – rectus femoris, vastus lateralis, vastus intermedius; gluteus medius and maximus

1 *With a barbell across your shoulders (front), squat as for a dumbbell squat.*

Wide-leg power squat

Muscles used Quadriceps – vastus medialis, rectus femoris, vastus lateralis and intermedius; gluteus medius and maximus; abductor magnus

1 *With a barbell across your shoulders (back), squat with your toes at 45 degrees.*

Machine hack squats

Muscles used Quadriceps – vastus medialis, vastus lateralis, rectus femoris

1 *Make sure that your back, shoulders, neck and head are fully supported. Place your feet shoulder-width apart in front of you.*

2 *Release the weight with the handle and squat down, keeping your back flat. With your feet shoulder-width apart, your knees won't go forward of your feet.*

3 *Once your thighs are parallel with the floor, pause for one second, then push the weight back up by straightening your legs.*

Leg press

Muscles used Quadriceps – vastus medialis, rectus femoris, vastus lateralis, vastus intermedius; gluteus maximus; biceps femoris – short head, long head

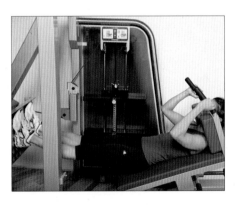

1 *Lie on the machine with your back resting against the back support. Place your feet hip-width apart against the foot support. Focus on tensing the abdominals so that you feel the burn more in that area. Push your weight through the heels to make the quadriceps work harder.*

2 *Carefully release the handle and slowly bend your legs, allowing the weight to come back toward you, until your legs are bent at 90 degrees at the knee. Push firmly down through the heels to get the quadricep muscles working really hard. Try to keep the head and neck relaxed, without any tension.*

3 *Pause for one second and then push the weight back away from you by extending your legs and pressing through your heels. To work your quadriceps, place your feet farther back on the foot plate. To work the hamstrings and gluteus maximus, place your feet farther up the plate.*

Leg Exercises: Quadriceps

The quadriceps are the large group of muscles at the front of your thighs. Leg extensions are the best way of isolating the quadriceps – and you can fully expect to feel as if your legs are on fire with the following leg extension exercises.

For each exercise, take 2 to 3 seconds for each movement. Breathe in at the start of the movement, and out as you return to the start position.

Basic leg extension

Muscles used Quadriceps – rectus femoris, vastus lateralis, vastus intermedius, vastus medialis

1 *Sit on the machine and tuck your legs behind the pad, which should rest just on the bottom of your shins. Sit upright, arms at the sides, and hold the handles to help keep your hips still.*

2 *To lift the weight up tense your quadricep muscles and fully extend the legs. Pause for 2 seconds, then slowly lower the weight back down. Get your legs back under you as far as possible.*

Machine single-leg extension

Muscles used Quadriceps – rectus femoris, vastus lateralis, vastus intermedius, vastus medialis

Exercises to build strong quadriceps	
Carry out these exercises in pairs and superset them so that you have just 5 to 10 seconds' rest between each set.	
Exercise	**Sets and repetitions**
Machine hack squat	5 x 8–12
Wide-leg power squat	5 x 8–12
Machine leg extension	5 x 8–12
Medialis leg extension	5 x 8–12

Sit comfortably, positioning yourself as you would for a basic leg extension. Lift the weight up by fully extending just one leg. Leave the other leg in the start position. Once the leg is horizontal, pause for 1 second and then slowly lower the weight back down. Keep the core tensed to prevent the body from twisting. This is an efficient way to make sure you get equal strength in both legs; it is also useful for rehabilitation purposes after an injury or an accident.

Medialis leg extension

Muscles used Quadriceps – vastus medialis, rectus femoris, vastus lateralis, vastus intermedius

1 *Position yourself as you would for a basic leg extension, hips still and legs tucked behind the pad, which should rest on the bottom of your shins. This extension aids knee injuries.*

2 *With your feet outward at 45 degrees, extend your legs to lift the weight. When your legs are straight, pause for 2 seconds, then slowly lower the weight. Emphasis is on the vastus medialis.*

Cable single-leg extension

Muscles used Quadriceps – rectus femoris, vastus lateralis, vastus intermedius, vastus medialis

1 *Attach the cable to the back of your lower leg. Stand facing away from the cable machine. Bring your knee up in front of you so that your leg is bent at 90 degrees. Keep your body still to keep the workload isolated on the quadriceps.*

2 *Tense your quadriceps and extend your leg until it is straight. Pause for 1 second and then slowly bend your knee back to the start position. Use a light weight to isolate your quadriceps or else the momentum will help to lift the weight.*

Cable hip flexor

Muscles used Tensor fascia lata; pectineus

1 *Attach the cable to the back of your lower leg, just above the ankle. Stand with your feet hip-width apart and your back to the cable machine. Tense your core muscles to keep your spine in neutral. Lift the leg that has the cable attached off the ground.*

2 *Bring your leg up in front of you, stretching it as far as it can go. Pause for 1 second then slowly lower the leg back down to the start position. Give the abdominals a good workout at the same time by tensing your abdominals to prevent your body from moving.*

Leg Exercises: General

The following exercises use the majority of the leg muscles; they simulate the same muscular movements that you make when you are running, walking or cycling. For athletes wishing to excel, these exercises should play a significant part in your training routine.

You don't have to be a highly competitive athlete to benefit from these exercises. These are also the exercises to do if you simply want to have firm buttocks. The human body – like many large, powerful animals – needs large gluteus muscles (buttocks) to provide power and speed. You don't actually need your gluteus muscles when you are just walking, but as soon as the intensity of the exercise increases, for example when you walk uphill or run, you need them to help extend your hip and keep an upright torso.

The exercises described here will help to train your gluteus muscles and work them in conjunction with your trunk and other lower-body muscles, which will improve your physical performance in your chosen sport.

Many people have weak gluteus muscles because of their sedentary lifestyle. They sit on these muscles but never use them. By putting one foot in front of the other, these exercises simulate everyday sporting movements, especially as they require balance that forces your smaller muscles to act as stabilizers and work in tandem with your core muscles. If the stabilizers around your trunk and lower-body muscles are inactive, you will be prone to injury as the intensity of your exercise increases.

For each exercise, take 2 to 3 seconds for each direction of the movement. Breathe in at the start of the movement, then breathe out as you return to the start position.

Exercises to build powerful buttocks	
Exercise	**Sets and repetitions**
Step-up	5 x 8–10
Bench drop lunge	5 x 8–10
Side lunge	5 x 8–10
Side step-up	5 x 8–10

Step-up

Muscles used Quadriceps – vastus medialis, rectus femoris, vastus lateralis, vastus intermedius; gluteus medius and maximus

1 *With a dumbbell in each hand, place one foot on the aerobics step (or bench). The slower you carry this out, the harder you work the quadriceps.*

2 *Step up to your full height. Hold the opposite foot in the air to work your leg harder. Pause for 1 second then slowly step back down.*

Side step-up

Muscles used Quadriceps – rectus femoris, vastus lateralis, vastus intermedius, vastus medialis; adductor – longus, magnus; gluteus medius and maximus

 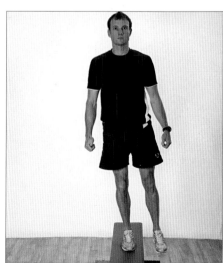

1 *Stand side-on to a bench (or aerobics step), with your arms by your side. Place the near foot on the bench.*

2 *Step up to your full height, pause, then slowly lower yourself back down, using your quadriceps to control the fall.*

Static lunge

Muscles used Quadriceps – rectus femoris, vastus lateralis, vastus intermedius, vastus medialis; gluteus maximus

1 *Stand with one foot in front of the other, roughly 60cm/2ft apart, with both feet facing forward, and your body weight suported evenly between your feet. Your back heel will be raised off the floor. Hold a dumbbell in each hand. Keep your hips level, your back straight and your shoulders back.*

2 *Slowly lower yourself by bending both legs until the thigh of your front leg is parallel with the floor. Pause for 1 second, then slowly push back up to the start position. Keep your chest out to help isolate the legs during the lunge.*

Bench drop lunge

Muscles used Quadriceps – rectus femoris, vastus lateralis, vastus intermedius, vastus medialis; gluteus maximus

1 *Standing with your back to a bench, with a dumbbell in each hand and your feet roughly 60cm/2ft apart, place one foot up on the bench behind you, with the top of the foot downward.*

2 *Slowly lower yourself by bending both legs until your front leg thigh is parallel with the floor. Try to get your back knee as low as possible for the best stretch. Pause for 1 second, then push back up.*

Side lunge

Muscles used Quadriceps – rectus femoris, vastus lateralis, vastus intermedius, vastus medialis; gluteus maximus and medius; adductor – longus, magnus; gracilis; pectineus

1 *Stand with your feet wide apart and your back straight. Keep your arms straight, your hands just touching the tops of your thighs. Hold a dumbbell in each hand. Keep your abdominals tensed all the time.*

2 *Lunge sideways, shifting your weight behind the bent leg, tensing the abdominals to support the lower back. With the thigh of the lunging leg parallel to the floor, pause for 1 second, extend the leg, then push yourself back to the start position.*

Leg Exercises: Hamstrings

The hamstrings are the group of muscles at the back of the thigh. Their function is to tip the pelvis back (posterior rotation) and straighten the pelvis when the pelvis is locked by isometric contraction – when the muscle exerts force but does not change in length.

Hamstrings are shortened by some exercises, such as cycling, and can often cause other muscles, such as those in the back and gluteus, to tighten. Hamstring injuries are also common. In runners, the hamstrings need to be long and stringy to allow a full range of movement. To achieve this, regular stretching when training hamstrings is essential. Take time to stretch after every set of hamstrings exercises to keep the muscles as long as possible.

If you get hamstring tears, stretch the muscle as soon as the pain has subsided to reduce the effect of the scar tissue, and re-educate the muscle to work with light hamstring exercises.

Sedentary lifestyles – which so many people lead today – make the hamstring muscles shorten, which leads to a curve in the lumbar region of the spine, making you prone to injury. If you have been sitting all day, make sure that you have at least 10 minutes of cardiovascular exercise and spend some time stretching to prepare your hamstrings for resistance training. Sportsmen and women often neglect their hamstrings, and the demands placed on them lead to muscle imbalances between the quadriceps and the hamstrings. The following exercises mainly work the hamstrings. Whatever your goal, you should try to train your hamstrings at least once a week.

For each exercise, take 2 to 3 seconds for each direction of the movement. Breathe in at the start of the movement, and breathe out as you return to the start position.

It can be difficult to recruit the hamstrings without using other muscles in the lower back. To prevent the lower back from working, tense your buttocks and pull in the abdominal muscles. If you suffer from lower-back pain, your hamstrings may be too tight and the abdominals cannot support your back. Try using lighter weights to prevent the muscles in your lower back recruiting.

Exercises to build indestructible hamstrings	
Exercise	**Sets and repetitions**
Machine leg curl	5 x 15–20
Seated leg curl	5 x 15–20
Lunge	5 x 15–20
Cable leg kickback	5 x 15–20

Machine leg curl

Muscles used Biceps femoris – short head and long head; semimembranosus; semitendinosus

1 Lie face down on the leg-curl machine with your legs tucked under the leg pad. Grip the handles and tense the core muscles to help maintain a still body and a neutral spine. Relax your head over the end of the bench or rest it to one side. The slower you do this exercise, the harder your hamstrings will have to work.

2 Gripping the handles firmly, curl the weight up until your legs are bent at 90 degrees. Tense your buttocks throughout the movement to help isolate your hamstrings and buttocks. Pause for 1 second in this position, then slowly lower the weight back down to the starting position.

Seated leg curl

Muscles used Biceps femoris – short head, long head; semimembranosus; semitendinosus

1 *Sit on the leg-curl machine with your back pressed firmly against the back pad for support. Tuck your legs under the top pad and rest them on the lower pad. Tense your core muscles to help maintain a still upper body, keeping your spine in neutral and your head facing forward, in line with your spine. Slightly point your toes to make the hamstrings work harder.*

2 *Pull up on the handles to keep the hips down in the seat. Curl the weight under you until your knees are bent at 90 degrees. Pause for a second, then return to the start position. Return to the start slowly so that your knees do not take all the weight, causing them to hyper-extend at the end of the movement.*

Cable single-leg curl

Muscles used Biceps femoris – short head, long head; semimembranosus; semitendinosus gastrocnemius – lateral head, medial head

1 *Face the cable machine with a strap around one ankle. Tense your core muscles to keep your spine in neutral, and keep your head facing forward in line with your spine. Hold the machine handles to help keep your torso still.*

2 *Curl the weight back behind you by bending at the knee until your leg is bent at 90 degrees. Pause for 1 second, then slowly straighten your leg to lower the weight back down to the start position.*

Cable leg kickback

Muscles used Gluteus maximus; gluteus medius; tensor fascia lata; biceps femoris – short head, long head

1 *Take up the same start position as for the cable single-leg curl (above) and tense your core abdominal muscles as much as possible to prevent your lower back from doing any of the work. Hold the machine handles for balance and to keep the torso still. The difference with this exercise is that it places more emphasis on your buttock muscles.*

2 *Tense your buttocks and kick the leg attached to the pulley back out behind you to 45 degrees. Pause for 1 second, then slowly return the leg to the start position. This is a great exercise for people who have weak buttocks, especially for runners or athletes who do not recruit their buttock muscles properly.*

Leg Exercises: Thigh Muscles

Working toward strong inner and outer muscles in the thighs can help maintain good balance and stabilize the knee joints, as well as keeping the leg bones aligned. It is best to build up gradually and stop exercising if any pain is experienced.

Whenever you start to accelerate with a longer stride or to lunge to one side, you are using your inner and outer thigh muscles. These muscles, which are known as the adductors and abductors, help to stabilize your body. For example, if you run and you have lots of lateral movement in the hips, it may cause a snaking effect in your spine, which can lead to back pain. In any case, you want to transfer all your power into going forward, not sideways. When riding a bike, you want all your leg power to go down through the chain to give you more forward speed. When hitting a golf ball, you want good hip stability to allow you to rotate and strike it with as much power and speed as possible.

The following exercises work a number of inner and outer thigh muscles together. There is no time for them to relax – when one is working, the other is acting as a stabilizer. While training these muscles, always contract your core muscles to help isolate the inner and outer thigh muscles you want to work. Be careful when starting your adductor and abductor routine. Begin with a light weight and work up. Don't ignore pain when training these muscles, as you could injure yourself.

For each exercise, take 2 to 3 seconds for each direction of the movement. Breathe in at the beginning of the movement, and breathe out as you return to the start position.

Exercise plan for abductor/ adductor strength and toning	
Exercise	**Sets and repetitions**
Lunge	3 x 20
Side lunge	3 x 20
Cable abduction	3 x 20
Cable adduction	3 x 20
Machine abduction	3 x 20
Machine adduction	3 x 20

Cable hip abduction

Muscle used Gluteus medius

1 *Stand side-on to the cable machine with feet hip-width apart. Attach an ankle strap to the outside leg. Keep the emphasis on the sides of the buttocks throughout the movement.*

2 *Slowly raise the outside leg as far out to the side as possible. Pause for a second, then slowly lower it back down. Doing the exercise slowly ensures that the gluteus is working hard.*

Cable adduction

Muscles used Adductor – longus, magnus; pectineus; gracilis

1 *Stand on one leg side-on to the cable machine. The other leg is raised in the air, attached to the cable by an ankle strap. Keep your upper body as still and upright as possible by tensing the abdominals.*

2 *Adduct the attached leg until the legs are together. Pause then lower the weight by taking your leg back out to the start. Start with a weight that is lighter than you think you can manage and then work your way upward.*

Machine abduction

Muscles used Gluteus – medius and maximus

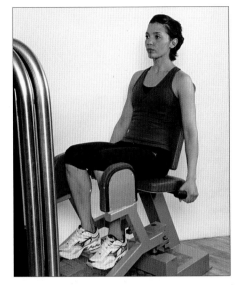

1 *Place your legs against the leg pads. Hold on to the handles to keep yourself firmly positioned in the seat. If you change the angle of your upper torso by adjusting the back pad angle you can focus the exercise on different muscles.*

2 *The more vertical the back pad, the more your gluteus maximus will work, and the more angled the back pad, the greater the emphasis on the gluteus medius. Tense your gluteus and spread the legs as far apart as comfortable. Pause for 2 seconds, then slowly bring your legs back together, while resisting the weight.*

Machine adduction

Muscles used Adductor muscles – brevis, longus, magnus; pectineus

1 *Place your legs into the leg pads and tense your core muscles to keep your torso motionless. Hold the handles to keep yourself in the seat while you do the exercise. Take this exercise slowly to begin with.*

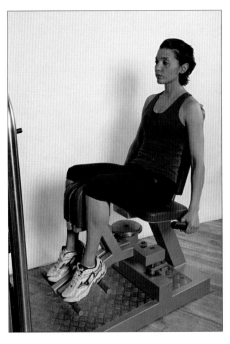

2 *Push in your legs until they meet. Pause for 2 seconds, then slowly allow them to be pulled back out, still tensing your muscles to create resistance. If you have never worked these muscles before, it will take some time to build them up.*

Elastic abduction

Muscles used Gluteus – medius, maximus

1 *Lie on your back with the legs bent up at 90 degrees and your feet flat on the floor in front of you. Place an elastic strip around your knees and tie it in a secure knot. Tense your abdominals so that you can keep your back flat on the floor.*

2 *In this exercise, to make your buttocks work even harder, do a hip raise before you move your legs apart. Tense the gluteus muscles and spread the knees as far apart as possible. Pause for 2 seconds, then slowly return to the start position, keeping the abdominals tense.*

Leg Exercises: Calf Muscles

Every time you step forward, you use your calf muscles. For faster activities, such as running and sprinting, strong calf muscles are essential. They maintain your forward motion and provide good strength and stability for the other muscles in your legs.

People often skip calf-strengthening exercises because they think they are dull. This is a mistake – you will not perform at your best with weak calves. Also, you will be prone to injury, particularly Achilles' injuries. Bodybuilders often say they can't be bothered with training their calves because they believe they can't build them up. The main reason for this is that calf muscles are small and it takes a lot of patience to see the gradual improvements in size and definition through the appropriate training. If this is the case for you, take time in your workout and make your calves a priority – even try putting calf exercises at the start of your workout for a few weeks.

Training the calf muscles

There are three muscles that flex and extend the foot to make up the calves. These are: the tibialis anticus, which runs down the front of the shin and contracts to flex the toes toward the knee; the gastrocnemius, a long, wide muscle that connects the bottom part of your upper leg to your heel (it flexes to extend your toes when your leg is straight and contracts to flex all of the muscles in the back of the leg); and the soleus, a shorter muscle that connects to the upper part of the shin and the heel, and works mainly when the leg is already bent at 90 degrees.

If you have been training your calves and seeing no improvement, try changing your routine. To get a better training effect, change the repetition range each time you train them. One day, do 6–10 reps with a heavier weight and, on another day, do 20–30 reps on a lighter weight. Try holding the weight for 3 seconds at the top of each peak contraction to make the calf muscles work even harder. But don't overtrain them and leave at least a day's rest between calf

sessions – otherwise your progress will come to a halt. Also, be careful not to train the calf muscles first if you also want to include bigger leg-muscle exercises in your routine. You need your calf muscles to be fresh if they are to provide enough support and stability when your bigger muscles are working.

Always stretch your calves to prevent them becoming tight and affecting the Achilles' tendon. If you do suffer from tight calves, do some regular stretching and have them massaged before this leads to injury. Stretching the calves can actually make them

Exercise plan for stronger calf muscles	
Exercise	**Sets and repetitions**
Double-leg calf raise	3 x 20
Calf press	3 x 20
Seated single-leg calf raise	3 x 20

bigger and give them a more ripped look. For each of these exercises, take 2 to 3 seconds to carry out each direction of the movement. Breathe in at the start of the movement, then breathe out as you slowly return to the start position.

Double-leg calf raise

Muscles used Triceps surae – gastrocnemius medial head, gastrocnemius lateral head, soleus

1 *Stand on the edge of a step on the balls of your feet. Hold on to the handles for balance. Tense your core muscles and the tops of your legs to keep your body in a straight line. Lower your heels below the line of the step.*

2 *Pause for a second, tense your calf muscles as much as possible and raise your heels as high as you can above the step. Pause for 2 seconds in this position, then lower yourself back down to the start position.*

Calf press

Muscles used Triceps surae – gastrocnemius medial head, gastrocnemius lateral head, soleus

1 *Sit in the calf-press machine, with the back straight and head in line. Hold the handles and place the balls of your feet up against the edge of the leg press plate. To put emphasis on the calf muscles, keep the whole leg as straight as possible and tense your core muscles to keep your back flat.*

2 *Keeping your calf muscles tense, press the plate away from you. Pause for 2 seconds, then slowly relax your calves. Repeat the exercise six to ten times. To make this exercise more demanding and to make sure you have equal strength in both legs, try using one leg only.*

Seated single-leg calf press

Muscles used Triceps surae – gastrocnemius medial head, gastrocnemius lateral head, soleus

1 *Sit in the calf-press machine, with the back straight. Hold the handles and place the balls of your feet up against the edge of the leg press plate. Straighten your legs and tense your core muscles to keep your back flat.*

2 *Take one leg off the plate, straighten the other, tense your core muscles and your calf muscle, and press the plate away from you. Pause for 2 seconds and slowly relax your calf. If you can do 50 repetitions, you have good calf strength.*

RESISTANCE TRAINING: UPPER BODY

Resistance training for the upper body helps to develop and strengthen the chest muscles using a variety of methods, such as bench presses and dumbbells and some just using your own body weight. Included are specific exercises to effectively work the back, shoulders, abdominals and arms. Getting fitter and stronger helps to strengthen the upper body for other sporting activities

Above: To build up your shoulder muscles, the dumbbell shoulder press is a useful exercise.
Left: The lat pull-down, wide grip trains the large back muscles.

Chest Exercises: Bench Press

The chest muscles are large muscles that cover the upper section of your ribs called the pectorals. They help to drag the upper arm forward via a tendon extending from the side of the upper arm bone to the pectoral muscle.

Bench pressing is the most common chest exercise and is a good exercise for building a bigger chest. There are several variations of the bench press that will help to tone and shape your pectorals. Bench press exercises, however, will only help build the lower and outer edges of the pectoral muscles.

To get the inner and upper parts of your chest working well, and give you good symmetry, you will need to do other exercises.

Top bodybuilders believe bench presses are the key to developing a strong, well-developed chest. There is no doubt that they do bring out the size in the chest and so it is no surprise that they are often referred to as the 'meat and drink' of all upper-body exercises.

Don't try to take the bar too low when doing the bench press or else other muscles will have to work, not just your chest muscles in isolation. Taking your elbows just past the line of your body is enough. As you press the weight back to the top, try to keep your chest as big as possible and force your pectorals to contract as much as possible.

Changing the angle of the position you are pressing from will help to work different parts of the chest. Putting the bench into an incline position will isolate the top part of the chest. It will also make the front of your shoulders work hard to create a strong connection between your chest and shoulders. Putting the bench into a decline bench position will work the lower part of your chest and your upper-back muscles, forcing a good connection between the chest and back muscles. If the bench press is going to be the biggest upper-body exercise in your routine, do it first, so that all your stabilizing muscles are fresh and can help support your chest muscles. Make sure it has been at least 48 hours since you last trained your triceps, because they can tire fast when you are doing bench presses.

For each exercise take 2 to 3 seconds for each direction of the movement. Breathe in at the beginning of the movement, and breathe out as you return to the start position.

Narrow grip bench press

Narrow grip bench press is a variation of the bench press. This involves holding the bar with your hands no more than 15cm/6in apart; this will work the inner pectorals and triceps.

Bench press exercises for bigger chest muscles

Exercise	Sets and repetitions
Incline press	5 x 6–8
Decline press	5 x 6–8
Bench press	5 x 6–8
Incline press	3 x 20+ less than 60 seconds' rest between sets
Decline press	3 x 20+ less than 60 seconds' rest between sets
Bench press	3 x 20+ less than 60 seconds' rest between sets

Bench press

Muscles used Pectorals major; anterior deltoid; triceps brachii – medial head and long head

1 *Lie on a bench with the head back and the feet on the floor. Grip the bar in both hands and hold it above you, in line with the middle of the chest. Grip it with your hands slightly wider than shoulder-width apart, palms facing outward. Keep the bar in line with your chest and not your shoulders or you might cause yourself an injury.*

2 *With straight arms, lower the bar down to your chest, bending your elbows to the side. Keep lowering until your elbows are at 90 degrees. Pause for 1 second, then raise the bar to the start position, keeping your abdominals tense. The bar should come down low enough to work your chest, and as you press it back up, push your chest out to make it work harder.*

Incline press

Muscles used Pectorals major; anterior deltoid; triceps brachii – medial head and long head

1 *Adjust the bench to a 45-degree incline. Lie on it and grip the bar, your palms facing your feet. Keep your feet flat on the floor. Hold the bar vertically above the top half of your chest. Rest your head on the bench and keep your back flat.*

2 *Lower the bar, taking your elbows out to the side until they are at 90 degrees. Pause for a second, then raise the bar to the start position. Tense your abdominals throughout the movement to help maintain a flat back.*

Decline press

Muscles used Pectorals major; triceps brachii – medial head, long head

1 *Adjust the bench to a 30-degree maximum decline. Lie on it with your legs hooked over the end to prevent sliding. Grip the bar with your palms facing toward your feet, your hands slightly wider apart than shoulder width. Hold the bar vertically above the lower half of your chest. Rest your head on the bench. This exercise is good for outlining the bottom of the chest. Keep the bar in line with the bottom of the chest and don't allow the shoulders to take over.*

2 *Gripping the bar firmly, lower it toward your chest, taking your elbows out to the side until they are at 90 degrees. Pause for 1 second, then raise the bar to the start position. Tense your abdominals throughout the movement to help maintain a flat back. Try to prevent your shoulders from rising up, which has the effect of tensing your neck muscles. In this way you will be able to place greater emphasis on your chest muscles.*

Chest Exercises: Dumbbell Presses

Dumbbell chest press exercises are similar to bench presses using the same muscles. However, you can go lower with dumbbells because there is no bar directly in front of the chest, thus providing a longer range of movement and a more intense workout for your chest.

The movement involved in dumbbell presses also enables the weight to progress from straight above the chest and out to the sides, making it a more effective exercise to develop the entire set of pectoral muscles.

Many bodybuilders believe they get faster results when they use dumbbells. Because dumbbells have to be balanced to carry out chest press exercises, this involves having to recruit all your stabilizing muscles so that you can control the movement of the dumbbells. As a result, your stabilizing muscles will develop better.

Always have a training partner with you when you are doing heavy dumbbell presses, as you can never tell when you may suddenly weaken, especially as one

arm might prove to be stronger than the other. (The dumbbells will reveal if one side of your body is weaker than the other.) Avoid big increases in weights to prevent injury and always be in control of the movement.

For each chest exercise, take 2 to 3 seconds for each direction of the movement. Don't forget your breathing: breathe in at the beginning of the movement and breathe out as you return to the start position.

> ### Chest building session for beginners
> Try doing supersets: pair up two exercises and switch from one exercise to the other with only 5–10 seconds' rest between sets. To get a really good workout, try doing the sets and repetitions twice weekly.
>
> | Exercise | Sets and repetitions |
> |---|---|
> | Bench press | 3 x 8–12 |
> | Dumbbell chest press | 3 x 8–12 |
> | Incline bench press | 3 x 8–12 |
> | Decline dumbbell press | 3 x 8–12 |

Dumbbell chest press

Muscles used Pectoralis major; triceps brachii; anterior deltoid

1 *Sit on the end of the bench with your feet firmly on the floor in front of you. Hold a dumbbell in each hand, resting on top of your thighs, palms facing toward each other. Keep the dumbbells in line with the middle of the chest. Slowly lie back, taking the dumbbells with you. Tense your abdominals to maintain a flat back.*

2 *Hold the dumbbells with straight arms above your chest, your palms facing your feet. Keep your feet on the floor, on the bench or in the air, with your legs at 90 degrees. Relax your head and rest it on the bench. Work the chest harder by pushing it out on the return phase. If you need to, rest in between chest presses.*

3 *Lower the weights, taking your elbows out to the side until they are at 90 degrees. To prevent injury, and isolate the chest and triceps, don't let your elbows go lower than 90 degrees. Raise the dumbbells to the position in step 2. The forearms should always be perpendicular to the ground. Continue with your planned repetitions.*

Incline dumbbell chest press

Muscles used Pectoralis major; triceps brachii – long head, medial head; anterior deltoid

1 *Adjust the bench to a 20- to 60-degree incline. Sit on the end of the bench with your feet on the floor. Hold a dumbbell in each hand, resting on your thighs, your palms facing toward each other. Tense your abdominals throughout the movement to help keep your back flat.*

2 *Lie back, placing your head on the bench, and hold the dumbbells with straight arms above the top half of your chest, with your palms facing feet. The raising movement here should be slightly rounded as if you are hugging a tree. Your back should be flat against the bench.*

3 *Lower the dumbbells, taking your elbows out to the side, keeping your forearms perpendicular to the ground, until your elbows are at 90 degrees. Pause for 1 second, then raise the dumbbells to the position in step 2. Keep them in line with the upper half of the chest for emphasis on the pectorals.*

Decline dumbbell chest press

Muscles used Pectoralis major; triceps brachii – long head, medial head

1 *Adjust the bench until it is at a 20- to 60-degree decline. Sit on the end of the bench with your feet placed firmly on the floor. Hold a dumbbell in each hand, resting on the top of your thighs, your palms facing toward each other. Lower yourself down slowly into the decline to give you an opportunity to work your abdominals.*

2 *Hold the dumbbells with straight arms above the lower half of your chest, with your palms facing your feet. Place the head against the bench and hook your legs over the end of the bench, or keep your legs straddling the bench, so that the feet are on the floor. Slowly raise the dumbbells upward above the upper chest so that the arms are straight.*

3 *Lower the dumbbells, taking the elbows out to the sides. Keep your forearms perpendicular to the ground, until your elbows are bent at 90 degrees. Pause for 1 second, then raise the dumbbells to the position in step 2. At the end of the movement, for more emphasis, squeeze the bottom of your pectorals up and together.*

Chest Exercises: Strength and Power

The following exercises will give you a strong powerful chest. They will also work the muscles that surround the chest and work alongside the pectorals. However, to get the results you want, you will need to do a range of chest exercises, not just one or two.

These exercises will work your chest muscles in conjunction with other surrounding muscles to make you more powerful for your chosen sport. Pullovers will make your abdominals and latissimus dorsi work hard to assist the chest muscles. It is also important to train your core muscles to recruit at the same time as your pectorals. If you are lifting heavy weights and your core strength is not working for you, you will be more prone to injuries and your chest will be useless in sporting movements.

Correct technique

Most of the following exercises force your arms to work independently and also engage your core so that you can actually do the exercise. The muscles surrounding your chest will work during these movements, give them the strength and tone to work in unison with your chest, and also improve your posture. It is easy to do other chest exercises with poor technique and get away with it. However, poor technique will quickly become apparent in these chest exercises because, quite simply, you won't be able to do them.

When you do your chest workout, concentrate and ensure you apply the correct muscles. Use a suitable weight when you do chest exercises. For each exercise, take 2 to 3 seconds for each direction of the movement. Breathe out at the start of the movement, and in as you return to the start position.

Chest stabilizing exercises	
Exercise	**Sets and repetitions**
Dumbbell chest press	3 x 12
Dip	3 x max
Dumbbell pullover	3 x 12
Machine pullover	3 x 12
Single-arm cable chest press	3 x 12
Medicine ball throw-down	3 x 12

Machine pullovers

Muscles used Pectoralis major; latissimus dorsi; teres major; serratus anterior; triceps brachii – long head

1 Sit in the pullover machine with your back against the back pad. Put your head flat against the back pad and tense your abdominals to keep your back flat.

2 Pull the handles over your head and out in front of you, bringing your hands level with your abdomen. Pause for 1 second, then return to the start position.

Dumbbell pullovers

Muscles used Pectoralis major; latissimus dorsi; teres major; serratus anterior; triceps brachii – long head

1 Lie with your shoulders resting on a bench, your feet on the floor, just over hip-width apart, and knees, hips and chest level with the bench. Hold a dumbbell above your chest with straight arms. Tense your core muscles throughout.

2 Lower the weight with straight arms until you feel the stretch in your chest. Don't make your back work, focus on the chest. Pause for 1 second, then return to the start. Keep your abdominals tight to maintain a straight body.

Dips

Muscles used Pectoralis major; anterior deltoid; triceps brachii – long head, lateral head and medial head

1 *Grip the handles and hold yourself up, with arms straight. Tense your core muscles to maintain a good position. Angle your head forward and down. To prevent the shoulders from rising upward, put greater emphasis on your chest.*

2 *Slowly lower your weight by bending your elbows out to the sides at 45 degrees, keeping them in line with your chest until your shoulders are level with your elbows. Lean slightly forward as you lower yourself. Once at 90 degrees pause for 1 second, then slowly return to the start position.*

Single-arm cable chest press

Muscles used Pectoralis major; latissimus dorsi; teres major; serratus anterior; triceps brachii – long head

1 *Face forward, core muscles tense, feet just wider than hip-width apart. Pull the handle forward until your elbow is at 90 degrees and in line with your body.*

2 *Pull the handle forward until your arm is straight and your hand is in front of your chest. Pause for 1 second, then return to the start position.*

Medicine ball throw-down

Muscles used Pectoralis major; latissimus dorsi; teres major; serratus anterior; triceps brachii – long head, medial head

1 *Stand with feet shoulder-width apart. Hold the medicine ball vertically above your head with straight arms.*

2 *Bring the medicine ball down in front of you to hit the floor fast enough to bounce back up above knee height.*

Chest Exercises: Pectorals

The inner and outer pectorals are possibly the hardest areas of the chest to work, and this usually involves pressing a weight above the chest at different angles. Some of the exercises described here use cables for a more effective workout.

Well developed pectoral muscles result from good upper and lower pectoral development.

More effective training

By using cables and changing the pressing action into a pulling action, you can make the training more effective for the inner and outer regions of the pectoral muscles. The cables provide a consistent tension through the entire range of the exercise, unlike a machine or free weights, which cannot work the chest in the same way. Instead of the weight attacking the chest muscle with gravity as, for example, in a chest press, with the cables the resistance is coming from the side of the chest.

People often find it difficult to get their chest to work to its full potential because they have weak triceps, which have to work with the chest in the pressing movement. But with these exercises, you hardly use your triceps. You can use these exercises at the start of your routine to pre-fatigue the pectoral muscles. Then you can do the other chest exercises with fresh triceps able to cope with the weights needed to make the chest burn – without the triceps weakening and letting you down. You can use dumbbells and the pec deck to similar effect – still not using your triceps. Take 2 to 3 seconds in each direction for each exercise. Breathe in as the weight is lowered, and out as you return to the start position.

Dumbbell flies

Muscle used Pectoralis major

1 *Lying back on the bench, with your feet on the floor, hold a dumbbell in each hand above your chest, with arms straight and your palms facing each other. You can keep your feet on the floor or on the bench. Push the chest out throughout to make it work harder.*

2 *Slowly lower the dumbbells to your sides in an arc, keeping your arms almost straight and in line with your chest. Once the dumbbells are level with the line of the body pause for 1 second, then slowly return to the start position.*

Incline dumbbell flies

Muscles used Pectoralis – major and minor

1 *With the bench inclined upward at a 30–60-degree angle, lie back, holding a dumbbell in each hand, with straight arms, above your chest, palms facing each other. Your feet can be on the floor or on the bench.*

2 *Slowly lower the dumbbells to the side of your body in an arc, keeping your arms almost straight and in line with the chest. Once the dumbbells are level with the line of the body, pause for 1 second, then return to the start position.*

Training plan for a ripped chest	
Exercise	**Sets and repetitions**
Dumbbell chest press	3 x 12
Dumbbell flies	3 x 12
Lying cable flies	3 x 12
Lower cable crossover	3 x 12
Pec deck	3 x 12

Low cable crossover

Muscles used Pectoralis – lower; triceps; biceps

1 *Stand with your feet facing forward, one behind the other. Grip the handles with palms facing forward and arms out at your sides at 180 degrees. Keep your core muscles working to maintain a still body position.*

2 *Keeping your arms almost straight (don't let the arms bend by more than 10 degrees), slowly pull your hands together and downward so that they meet in front of your chest. Pause for 1 second, then slowly let the weight pull your hands back to the start position, squeezing the lower part of the chest as you return to the start position.*

Lying cable flies

Muscles used Pectoralis – major, minor

1 *Lie on the bench and grip the handles with your palms facing each other. Keep your arms straight and in line with your chest.*

2 *Slowly let the weight pull your arms apart until your elbows are level with your chest. Pause for 1 second, then slowly return to the start position.*

Pec deck

Muscle used Pectoralis major

1 *Sit with your back flat against the support, feet on the floor, elbows and forearms resting against the pads, elbows at 90 degrees, in line with the bottom of your chest. Start with your arms out in front, the pads almost touching. Keep your head in line with your spine. Try to keep a relaxed grip throughout.*

2 *Slowly let the weight pull the arms back until they are level with your body. Pause for 1 second before pulling your arms back to the start position, pushing through your elbows and forearms to work the chest. Tense the abdominal muscles to maintain a flat back throughout the movement.*

Chest Exercises: Body Weight-training

There are a variety of chest exercises you can perform using just your body weight. The principal advantage is that you can retain the firm chest you developed in the gym even when you are on holiday or travelling on business.

It is possible to work your chest muscles without going to the gym, and simple press-ups are very effective. Press-ups from different angles work different parts of the pectoral muscles and can be incorporated into outdoor workouts using park benches. To work the stabilizing muscles surrounding your chest harder, use fit balls and medicine balls.

For each exercise, take 2 to 3 seconds for each direction of the movement. Breathe in at the start of the movement and out as you return to the start position.

Press-up

Muscles used Pectoralis major; anterior deltoid; triceps brachii – medial head, long head

1 *Place your hands on the floor, just over shoulder-width apart, your feet behind you, hip-width apart, elbows in line with your chest. Tense your core muscles and keep your head in line with your spine.*

2 *Keeping your abdominals tight, lower yourself toward the floor, taking your elbows out to the side until your chest is one fist from the floor. Pause for a second, then return to the start position.*

Decline press-up

Muscles used Pectoralis major; triceps brachii – medial head and long head

1 *Place your hands on the floor, just over shoulder-width apart, core muscles tense, feet behind you on the bench, hip-width apart, elbows in line with your chest. Keep your head in line with your spine.*

2 *Lower yourself toward the floor, taking your elbows out to the side until your chest is one fist from the floor. Pause for a second, then return to the start position.*

Incline press-up

Muscles used Pectoralis major; anterior deltoid; triceps brachii – medial, long head

This is a simple variation on the standard press-up. The start position is exactly the same except that you place your hands on an aerobic step instead of on the floor. Then lower yourself toward the step, taking your elbows to the side. Pause for 1 second, then return to the start position. To make sure that your chest does the work, don't push back behind you, and keep your chest up above the bench. Keep the core muscles tensed to hold the straight body position throughout the movement.

Knee press-up

If you haven't done press-ups before, don't press up completely from your arms, start by doing them balancing on your knees. Gradually increase the angle at the back of your knees as you get stronger and can support yourself fully on your arms. This method is recommended for women.

Fit ball press-up

Muscles used Pectoralis major; anterior deltoid; triceps brachii; serratus anterior; abdominals; gluteus

1 *Place your hands on the fit ball. Keep your arms straight, your feet behind you, hip-width apart, and your head in line with your spine. Tense your core muscles to keep your body straight. Turn your hands outward at 45 degrees to avoid wrist injuries.*

2 *Slowly lower your weight, taking your elbows out to the side until they are bent at 90 degrees. Pause for 1 second, then return to the start. Take extra care, or avoid this exercise if you have weak wrists.*

Chest exercises with little equipment	
Exercise	**Sets and repetitions**
Double-hand medicine ball press-up	3 x 10
Single-hand medicine ball press-up	3 x 10
Decline press-up	3 x 10
Press-up	3 x max
Incline press-up	3 x max

Single-hand medicine ball press-up

Muscles used Pectoralis major; triceps brachii; abdominals

1 *Place one hand on the ball and one hand on the floor, just wider than shoulder-width apart. Your wrist should be in the middle of the top of the ball to prevent wrist injuries. Support your weight on straight arms, your feet out behind you, hip-width apart. Keep your elbows in line with your chest. Use your core muscles to maintain this position. Your head should remain in line with your spine throughout the movement.*

2 *Keeping the core muscles switched on to maintain good balance and posture, slowly lower your body weight, taking your elbows out to the side until they are at 90 degrees. Pause for 1 second before returning to the start position. Keep your abdominal muscles tight throughout the movement to maintain a straight body. As you get stronger, transfer more weight onto the side with the medicine ball so your muscles work harder and improve your stability.*

Double-hand medicine ball press-up

Muscles used Pectoralis major; triceps brachii – medial, long and lateral heads

1 *Place both hands on the ball. Support your weight on straight arms, and keep your feet out behind you, hip-width apart, with the toes on the floor and the heels raised. Keep your elbows in line with your chest. Switch on your core muscles to maintain good balance and posture. Your head should remain in line with your spine throughout the movement.*

2 *Keeping your core muscles tense, slowly lower yourself, taking your elbows out to the side until they are at 90 degrees. The angle of the elbows changes the emphasis of the exercise. The closer your elbows are to your ribs the more the triceps will work, the farther away, the harder the chest muscles will work. Pause for 1 second before returning to the start position.*

Back Exercises: The Lats

Your back is one of the strongest areas of your body but one that is often neglected by gym users. This may be because it is difficult to see the back muscles, which makes it harder to monitor them, and therefore to stay motivated to train them.

The following exercises work the large muscles called latissimus dorsi, which are situated on the widest part of the upper back. For each exercise, take 2 to 3 seconds for each direction of the movement. Breathe out at the beginning of the movement, and breathe in as you return to the start position. Try using forced repetitions, when you have done as many reps as possible. Get your training partner to help you do two to three more reps.

Exercises to build stronger back muscles

The back muscles are large, so it takes hard work to train them.

Exercise	Sets and repetitions
Overhand chin-up	5 x max
Lat pull-down, wide grip	3 x 12
Lat pull-down, underhand grip	3 x 12

Lat pull-down, wide grip

Muscles used Latissimus dorsi; teres major; biceps brachii; brachialis

1 Hold the bar using a wide overhand grip. Sit on a seat, bench, fit ball or floor. Place your feet on the floor between you and the machine, shoulder-width apart. Lean back slightly and keep your head in line with your spine. Keep your body fixed in one position with your abdominals tensed.

2 Pull the bar toward the bottom of your chest, your elbows going out to the side and behind you. When the bar is close to the chest, pause for 1 second, then slowly return to the start position. Push your chest out as the bar is pulled in. Focus on using your lat muscles and don't let your shoulders rise up in the movement.

Lat pull-down, underhand grip

Muscles used Latissimus dorsi; teres major; biceps brachii; brachialis

1 Sit on the bench, with your feet shoulder-width apart, between you and the machine. Hold the bar with a close underhand grip. Lean back slightly and keep your head in line with the spine.

2 Pull the bar toward the bottom of your chest, chest out, elbows out to the side and behind you. When the bar is close to your chest, pause for a second, then slowly return to the start position.

Overhand chin-up, wide grip

Muscles used Latissimus dorsi; teres major; rhomboid – minor, major; biceps brachii; brachialis

1 *Grip the outside of the chin-up bar with an overhand grip so that your palms are facing away from you. Hang from the bar with straight arms and tense core muscles. Keep your head facing forward and in line with your spine. Your legs should be hanging straight under you in line with your body.*

2 *Slowly pull your body weight up, with your elbows going out to the sides until your chin is over the top of the bar. Pause for 1 second, then return to the start position. Keep the core muscles tensed at all times, and let your arms go almost straight between repetitions.*

Rope pull-down

Muscles used Latissimus dorsi; teres major; biceps brachii; brachialis

1 *Hold the rope using a wide overhand grip. Place your feet on the floor, shoulder-width apart, between you and the machine. Lean back slightly and keep your head in line with your spine. Don't let the weight drag you forward and round your shoulders.*

2 *Pull the rope toward the bottom of your chest, chest out and elbows to the side and behind you. Push your hips slightly forward and tense your core muscles to emphasize your lats. When the rope is close to your chest, pause for a second, then slowly return to the start.*

Straight arm cable pull-down

Muscles used Latissimus dorsi; teres major; triceps brachii – long head

1 *Face the cable machine with feet shoulder-width apart. Hold the bar in front of you at eye level, with straight arms. Tense the core muscles during the exercise. Keep your head in line with your spine during the movement.*

2 *Pull the bar down to below the waist. Keep the grip relaxed so the back, abdominals and triceps work harder. Pause for 1 second, then return to the start. Push the chest out and keep the head facing forward throughout.*

Back Exercises: The Spine

The following exercises will work all the major muscles of your back, but with greater emphasis on the muscles close to the spine. These are excellent exercises to strengthen your back for sports such as rowing and sailing.

Many people avoid training their back muscles because it is so energy intensive. But back muscles, alongside thigh and buttock muscles, are the largest in the body, so it is worthwhile training them properly. You should feel breathless at the end of a set of back exercises because these large muscles use a lot of oxygen.

Most back exercises involve pulling a weight toward you and demand a certain amount of bicep and forearm strength. To get the best training effect, do your back exercises first and arms later – otherwise your arm muscles will not be able to support the heavy weights you need to work the back muscles hard.

For each exercise, take 2 to 3 seconds during each direction of the movement. Breathe out at the beginning of the movement; breathe in as you return to the start position.

Exercises for a wider, V-shaped back	
Exercise	**Sets and repetitions**
Overhand chin-up, wide grip	3 x max
Lat pull-down, wide grip	3 x 12
Seated cable row	3 x 12
Single-arm dumbbell row	3 x 12
Single-arm cable row	3 x 12

Single-arm cable row

Muscles used Latissimus dorsi; teres major; rhomboid major; trapezius; posterior deltoid; biceps brachii; brachialis; brachioradialis

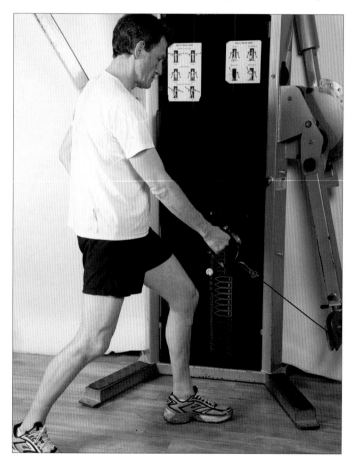

1 *Stand firm, with one foot in front of the other, 60cm/2ft apart. Keep your body square on, to isolate the muscles that should be used. Reach down, grip the handle and pull it up with a straight arm to the start position. Lean forward, toward the machine, placing your spare hand on the machine to help keep your body still.*

2 *Do not use a weight that is so heavy that your back has to twist to help your arm pull it in. Pull the handle toward your armpit, allowing your elbow to pass close to your ribs, and back behind you. Do not let your shoulder rise up in the movement. Pause for 1 second, then slowly let the handle return to the start position, keeping your feet firmly in place.*

Single-arm cable row, high to low

Muscles used Latissimus dorsi; teres major; rhomboid minor; rhomboid major; biceps brachii; brachialis; brachioradialis

1 *Stand with one foot in front of the other, 60cm/2ft apart, to establish a good base. Reach down and grip the handle and pull it up with a straight arm to the start position. Single-arm rows are one of the best exercises for the shoulder and upper back.*

2 *Stand up and lean slightly backward, with your pelvis pushed slightly forward. Start with the cable in a higher position and pull it down with your elbow, brushing past your ribs. Repeat the exercise using the other arm. This exercise helps if there is poor posture as a result of weakness of the muscles at the back of the shoulders and upper back.*

Single-arm dumbbell row

Muscles used Latissimus dorsi; teres major; rhomboid major; trapezius; posterior deltoid; biceps brachii; brachialis; brachioradialis

1 *Place your left knee and left hand on a flat bench. Keep your right foot on the ground, with your leg straight, and position yourself with your back parallel to the bench. Grip the dumbbell in your right hand with a straight arm. Tense your core muscles to maintain this position. Keep your core muscles working hard to stop your back twisting.*

2 *Pull the weight up, allowing your elbows to pass close to your ribs, and back behind the line of your body, until your hand is just under your armpit. If your body can't stay square-on to the bench, then you know the weight is too heavy. Pause for 1 second, then slowly lower the weight back to the start position.*

Seated cable row

Muscles used Rhomboid major; teres major; latissimus dorsi; trapezius; erector spinae; posterior deltoid; biceps brachii; brachialis; brachioradialis

1 *Sit on the floor, legs almost straight out in front of you, your feet up against the machine or foot rests. Keeping both arms and your back straight, and abdominals tensed, pull the handles back with both hands. Keep the chest pushed out throughout the movement so that the shoulders stay behind the line of the chest.*

2 *Pull the handles toward you, allowing your elbows to pass close to your ribs until the handles are near to your armpits. Pause for 1 second, then let the handles slowly return to the start position. Tense the core muscles and don't let your shoulders get dragged forward as the weight returns to the start position.*

Back Exercises: Back Muscles

For these exercises, you will need you to recruit your core muscles more than ever, as they form a strong connection between the upper and lower body. If you want to build body mass and pure lifting strength, these are the right exercises for you.

The following exercises work all the back muscles. They may be of particular use to you for lifting heavy weights and in contact sports such as rugby and American football. These exercises are exhausting, as you use a massive amount of muscle. So, practise getting your breathing right to ensure you are getting enough oxygen to your muscles, especially as you are trying to tense the core muscles as much as possible throughout the movements.

Make sure that you do at least 10 minutes' cardiovascular exercise and some stretching before you start these exercises, to get good blood flow to the muscles and avoid injury. Practise without any weight to get the correct technique before adding weights.

For each exercise, take 2 to 3 seconds for each direction of the movement. Breathe out at the beginning of the movement, and in as you return to the start position.

Exercises to build mass for your back	
Exercise	**Sets and repetitions**
Olympic bar deadlift	3 x 8–10
Single-arm dumbbell row	3 x 8–10
Bent-over barbell row	3 x 8–10
Underarm barbell row	3 x 8–10
Seated cable row	3 x 8–10

Olympic bar deadlift

Muscles used Trapezius; rhomboid major; latissimus dorsi; gluteus maximus; semitendinosus; semimembranosus; biceps femoris – long head and short head; vastus lateralis, medialis; rectus abdominis

1 *Stand with your feet shoulder-width apart. Bend your knees until your thighs are nearly parallel with the floor, the upper body leaning forward, bending at the hip. Arch your lower back slightly and tense your core muscles as much as possible. They must remain tight throughout this exercise in order to prevent your back from becoming rounded. A rounded back could result in severe spinal disc problems. Look straight ahead, keeping your head in line with the spine.*

2 *Grip the Olympic bar with an overhand grip, with palms facing backward. The hands should be shoulder-width apart, arms straight. Pull the weight up by straightening your legs, with the bar passing close to your shins and over the knees in a smooth, continuous movement. Straighten your upper body until you are completely upright. Pause for 1 second, then slowly reverse the movement back to the start position.*

Bent-over barbell row

Muscles used Latissimus dorsi; teres major; rhomboid major; trapezius; posterior deltoid; biceps brachii; brachialis; brachioradialis

1 Grip the bar with an overhand grip, hands just wider than shoulder-width apart. Bend your hips at just 90 degrees. With your feet shoulder-width apart, legs straight and core muscles tensed, push your hips back and arch your lower back slightly to maintain good body position. The bar should hang, from straight arms, perpendicular to the ground.

2 Pull the bar toward your chest, with your elbows going out to the sides until the bar is against your chest. Pause for 1 second, then lower the weight back to the start position.

Bench barbell row

Muscles used Latissimus dorsi; teres major; rhomboid major; trapezius; posterior deltoid; biceps brachii; brachialis; brachioradialis

Lie face down on the bench with your abdominals tensed to provide a stable base. Grip the bar using an overhand grip just over shoulder-width apart. Pull the bar up toward you with the elbows passing your ribs at the sides. Once at the top pause for a second and then slowly lower the bar back down. Keep arms straight to work the back muscles through a range of movement.

Bent-over T-bar row

Muscles used Posterior deltoid; teres – minor, major; trapezius; infraspinatus; rhomboid; latissimus dorsi; erector spinae; brachialis; brachioradialis

1 Stand with your legs either side of the T-bar, shoulder-width apart. Grip the bar with an overhand grip, slightly bend your knees and bend your upper body at the hips, keeping your torso very still.

Underarm barbell row

Muscles used Latissimus dorsi; teres major; rhomboid major; trapezius; posterior deltoid; biceps brachii; brachialis; brachioradialis

The start position is the same as for the bent-over barbell row (left), except you grip the bar with an underhand grip, hands just wider than shoulder-width apart. Bend the hips at 90 degrees. With your feet shoulder-width apart, legs straight and core muscles tensed, push the hips back and arch your lower back slightly to maintain good body position. The bar hangs perpendicular to the ground.

2 Pull the bar in toward your body, with your elbows bending out to the side, behind the line of your body. Once the bar is close to your ribs, pause for a second, then return to the start position.

Shoulder Exercises: General

Many people want wider shoulders. Although you can't increase the actual bone size of the shoulder, you can, with the right exercises, increase your shoulder muscle, which will make your shoulders appear much broader.

For most people, changing the width and depth of their shoulders makes them appear different and can have a dramatic effect on their body shape. Wider shoulders make it much easier to give your torso a great V-shape. Hanging clothes on wide shoulders can make you look more athletic and slimmer.

There are a number of shoulder exercises that you can use to build the depth and increase the width of your shoulder muscles.

To build strong shoulders, you need to use three types of movement: pressing, pulling and raising. It can take a long time to develop really strong shoulders because there are a number of different muscles surrounding a complex joint, and these are not necessarily muscles you use in everyday life.

Your deltoid is the primary muscle in your shoulder and is split into three parts: the anterior deltoid, medial deltoid and posterior deltoid. Depending on the movement you are performing, one part of the deltoid will work more than the others. In most movements, however, two parts of the deltoid will work together, or even all three parts. Make sure that you use the correct weight and warm up sufficiently in order not to damage the smaller muscles in the shoulder (rotator cuff).

When you start training your shoulders, it is important that you use basic pressing exercises to make your shoulder muscle active before moving on to exercises better suited for isolating the different areas of the shoulder. Otherwise, you might injure yourself.

Make sure your lower back is well supported during any pressing movements. As soon as you feel your body starting to twist while trying to do shoulder exercises, your shoulders are fatigued and you should rest. For every exercise, take 2 to 3 seconds for each direction of the movement. Breathe out at the beginning of the movement and in as you return to the start position.

Exercises to build stronger shoulders for beginners	
Exercise	Sets and repetitions
Olympic bar front shoulder press	3 x 12
Dumbbell shoulder press	3 x 12
Alternate dumbbell shoulder press	3 x 20

Olympic bar front shoulder press

Muscles used Deltoid – middle, anterior, posterior; triceps brachii – medial head, lateral head and long head

1 *Sit on the bench with your back pushed against the pad and put your feet out in front of you, shoulder-width apart, for support. If possible, put your feet up against a wall or dumbbell rack to help keep your back flat. Grip the bar firmly with both hands using an overhand grip. Always have someone there to spot for you for this exercise.*

2 *Lift the bar from the rack up above your head and hold it in a straight-arm position. Slowly lower the bar down, with the elbows going out to the sides, until the bar is in front of your head at eye level. Pause for 1 second, then press the bar back up to the start position. Take care, the shoulders can fatigue, so that you struggle to get the bar back on the rack.*

Dumbbell shoulder press

Muscles used Deltoid – middle, anterior, posterior; triceps brachii

1 *Sit on the bench with your feet in front of you, shoulder-width apart, to make a firm base. Slowly lift the weights up above your shoulders until they are straight up above head height, out to the sides. Try not to let your neck tense, and keep your shoulders working equally.*

2 *Slowly lower the weights, with your elbows going out to the sides to 90 degrees, the weights level with your ears. Pause for 1 second, then press the weights back up to the start position.*

Alternate shoulder press

Muscles used Deltoid – middle, anterior, posterior; triceps brachii – medial head, lateral head and long head

1 *Sit on the bench, feet out in front of you or pressed up against a wall or dumbbell rack, at least shoulder-width apart, to make a firm base. Keep your core muscles tight throughout the movement. With one arm, lift one weight above your shoulders until it is straight up above head height, out to the side. Move slowly, without jerking, so you don't damage any muscles.*

2 *Slowly lower the weight, with your elbow going out to the side, until it is at 90 degrees and the dumbbell is level with your ears. Pause for 1 second, then press the weight back up to the start position. Repeat with the other side. Wait for one arm to complete the press before you start to press the dumbbell up with the other arm.*

Body weight shoulder press

Muscles used Deltoid – middle, anterior, posterior; pectoralis major; triceps brachii – medial head, lateral head, long head

1 *Assume the decline press-up position with your feet up behind you on a bench. Pike at the hips and bring your hands back closer toward you, palms flat on the floor. Avoid this exercise if you have weak wrists.*

2 *Lower yourself down by bending your elbows until your head is almost touching the floor. Try not to let your back arch. Pause for 1 second, before pressing back up to the position in step 1.*

Shoulder Exercises: Rotational Strength

The following exercises will work the shoulder muscles as well as some of the muscles surrounding them. The range of movement involved will make your core and stabilizing muscles work harder, giving you the benefits of good rotational strength.

Most sports require some rotation at the shoulder joint. Throwing movements use all the muscles in the deltoid and make you over-dominant in one arm, which can lead to muscle imbalances and injury. So it is important that you work both shoulder muscles equally. In these rotational movements, many shoulder muscles have to work together. The rotator cuff, often the site of shoulder injuries, is the main stabilizer during any shoulder movement to keep the ball of the upper arm central. If it is not centred, this can put abnormal stress on the surrounding tissue, making tendonitis, rotator cuff tears and shoulder impingement likely.

As you get older, the tendons in the rotator cuff lose elasticity, making injury more likely. With age, too, comes a gradual decline in the muscle bulk that surrounds the shoulder. The following exercises will help to counteract the effect of aging, allowing you to continue with your chosen sport for longer.

The rotator cuff is made up of three parts: the supraspinatus, located at the top of the shoulder, which adducts the shoulder (raises the upper arm and moves it away from the body); the subscapularis, at the front of the shoulder, which internally rotates the shoulder; and the infraspinatus and teres, at the back of the shoulder, which externally rotates it. The following exercises work all three.

Generally, take 2 to 3 seconds for each direction of the movement. Breathe out at the beginning of the movement, and in as you return to the start position.

Cable shoulder press

Muscles used Deltoid – middle, anterior, posterior; triceps brachii – medial head, lateral head and long head

1 *Stand with your feet shoulder-width apart, one foot in front of the other and hold the handles at shoulder height.*

2 *Press the handles above your head until your arms are straight. Pause for a second, then slowly lower the weight back down.*

Variation: single-arm cable shoulder press

Muscles used Deltoid – middle, anterior, posterior; triceps brachii – medial head, lateral head and long head

Start by holding one handle of the cable shoulder press above your head until your arm is straight. Pause for 1 second then slowly lower the weight back to the start. Repeat with the other arm.

Exercises to build rotational strength of shoulders

Try some forced sets on the final exercise by getting your partner to help you with the lat two reps after you have already fatigued.

Exercise	Sets and repetitions
Arnie shoulder press	3 x 12
Cable shoulder press	3 x 12
Single-arm shoulder press	3 x 12
Olympic bar front shoulder press	3 x 8–12

Seated reverse dumbbell shoulder press, with rotation

Muscles used Deltoid – middle, anterior, posterior; pectoralis major; triceps brachii – medial head, lateral head and long head

1 *Sit on the bench, with core muscles tense. Bring the dumbbells up in front of your shoulders, palms facing you and your elbows as close together as possible.*

2 *Press the dumbbells upward, palms facing you and elbows as close together as possible. As the dumbbells reach eye level, start to rotate them so that they have rotated through 180 degrees by the time they reach the straight-arm position above your head. Pause at the top, then slowly lower the weights, rotating back to the start position.*

Arnold shoulder press

Muscles used Deltoid – middle, anterior, posterior; pectoralis major; triceps brachii – medial head, lateral head and long head; biceps brachii; brachialis; brachioradialis

1 *Use a lighter weight than you think you need to keep the emphasis on the deltoids. Stand with the feet shoulder-width apart. Hold one dumbbell in each hand, your arms by your sides, your hands just below hip level.*

3 *Keeping your palms facing toward you and your elbows close together, press the dumbbells up to eye level before rotating them through 180 degrees to complete the press-up above your head. At the top, pause for a second before slowly lowering the dumbbells, and gradually rotating them through 180 degrees.*

2 *Slowly bicep-curl the dumbbells by bending the elbow until the dumbbells are at shoulder height, with your elbows squeezed into your ribs. Keep your head and back straight and avoid arching the back.*

4 *As you complete the 180-degree rotation on the way back down, reverse-curl the dumbbells to the start position. For this exercise, take 4 to 5 seconds in each direction. Don't let the back arch during this exercise. Keep your abdominals tensed throughout the entire movement. If you feel your upper torso twisting, stop immediately.*

Shoulder Exercises: Connecting the Muscles

To make the connection between your deltoids, trapezius and other upper back muscles stronger, these exercises are essential. For the deltoids, the main emphasis will be on the anterior and medial deltoid muscles.

As these exercises require you to lift your shoulders upward, it is important to keep your neck relaxed to prevent injury and to keep the emphasis on the appropriate muscles. If you are involved in contact sports, these exercises are essential to provide the strength you need in the shoulders, upper back and neck. For combat sports, such as boxing, exercising these muscles should also be a priority.

The deltoids move the upper arm in a number of directions and are split into three parts called heads: the anterior head at the front of the shoulder; the medial head in the middle of the shoulder; and the posterior head at the rear of the shoulder. If you look at a bodybuilder from above, you should be able to see all three parts clearly defined like strips of muscle wrapped around the shoulder. Depending on the direction of the shoulder movement, one of the heads of the shoulder will work harder than the others to achieve the correct movement.

If you raise your arm up in front of you from down by your side, you will make the anterior head work the hardest. Raising your arm out to the side will work the medial head the hardest. Pulling your arm back behind you will work the posterior head. Most movements will work two of the heads – and sometimes three.

Be careful with the following exercises not to use your body weight to move the weights. It is easy to arch your back or bend the legs in the last few reps to make lifting the weights easier. Upright rowing exercises greatly exert the upper back and the trapezius muscles, which is good as long as your lower back is not doing the work. If you find it hard to prevent your body arching backward, try positioning yourself with one foot in front of the other to create a more stable platform, and tense your core muscles to restrict how far you can lean back.

For each exercise, take 2 to 3 seconds for each direction of the movement. Breathe out at the beginning of the movement, and in as you return to the start position.

Exercises for shoulder muscles	
Exercise	**Sets and repetitions**
Dumbbell shoulder press	3 x 12
Arnie shoulder press	3 x 12
Upright cable row	3 x 12
Upright dumbbell row	3 x 12
Dumbbell shoulder shrug	3 x 12

Upright cable row

Muscles used Trapezius; deltoids – anterior, posterior

1 *Stand 60cm/2ft from the cable machine, with your feet shoulder-width apart. Grip the bar with an overhand grip, with hands thumb-width apart. Tense your core muscles to help keep your back straight throughout the movement. Try to keep your neck relaxed throughout the movement.*

2 *Pull the bar up toward your chin, and take your elbows out to the sides, keeping them above the wrists throughout the movement. Once the bar is at chin height, pause for 1 second, then slowly lower the bar back down to the start position. Try not to lean backward as you start to fatigue.*

Above: With a contact sport such as boxing, shoulder exercises are necessary for strength in the neck, shoulders and upper back.

Upright dumbbell row

Muscles used Trapezius; deltoids – middle, anterior, posterior

1 *Stand with feet shoulder-width apart. Grip the dumbbells with an overhand grip, with palms facing backward. Hold the dumbbells with your arms straight down in front of you. Tense your core muscles to keep your back straight. Your head should be in line with your spine. Ask your training partner to monitor your technique and make sure that you are not tensing your neck.*

2 *Pull the dumbbells up, taking your elbows out to your side until the dumbbells are level with your chin. Keep hands close together throughout the movement. Keep the elbows above your wrists at all times. Try to keep the neck relaxed to help isolate the shoulders. Once you reach chin level, pause for 1 second then lower the dumbbells back down to the start position.*

Dumbbell shoulder shrug

Muscles used Trapezius; deltoids – middle, anterior, posterior

1 *Stand with your feet shoulder-width apart and your arms hanging straight by your sides to just below hip level. Grip one dumbbell in each hand, with your palms facing inward. Try to avoid tensing your neck.*

2 *Keeping your arms as straight as possible, lift the outside of the shoulders up to raise the dumbbells just a few centimetres. Pause for 1 second, then lower the weights back down to the start position.*

Shoulder Exercises: The Anterior Deltoids

The exercises here train the front of the shoulders (anterior deltoids), with little strength coming from other parts of your deltoids. These muscles give you toned shoulders and are essential for exercises, especially those involving pressing big weights above the chest.

The anterior deltoid muscles are involved in stabilizing the muscles during chest presses and are heavily involved when a chest exercise is done on an incline. The high usage of this muscle makes it susceptible to injury. It is a mistake to try to work these muscles using shoulder exercises in the same routine as chest presses or even on the day after. You must try to avoid overtraining the anterior deltoids, so have a day's rest between exercises that involve using them.

All these exercises involve raising movements, so there will be no real help from your triceps. People often choose to work the anterior deltoids harder than other parts of the deltoids because it is easy to see the muscle in the mirror. But this often leads to muscle imbalances and can make the anterior deltoids over-dominant in the movement of the shoulder press exercises, causing the weight to be dragged forward. Your posture will also be affected in that your shoulders will be dragged forward, creating a more rounded upper back. Make sure you balance this out by using the other parts of the deltoid. If you

have poor posture, you need to pay more attention to exercising the medial and posterior deltoid in your workouts. It is worth considering omitting specific exercises for these muscles from your routine, because they will be worked with the chest press exercises anyway.

When planning your routine, make sure that you use each arm equally to prevent one getting stronger than the other. To help isolate the muscle, try

sitting down for some of the exercises in order to prevent your body getting into too much of a swinging motion. You may need to use a lighter weight than you think you need so that you will be able to activate the muscle correctly.

For each exercise, take 2 to 3 seconds for each direction of the movement. Breathe out at the beginning of the movement, and in as you return to the start position.

Single-arm dumbbell frontal raise

Muscles used Deltoids – middle, anterior, posterior; pectoralis major

1 *Stand with your head up but relaxed, and your feet shoulder-width apart so that you feel stable and balanced. Take hold of a dumbbell in each hand and hold them close together in front of your thighs, with your arms hanging straight down and the palms facing behind you.*

2 *Pull one arm forward, keeping it straight, until it is in front of you at eye level. Try not to let momentum take over. Pause for 1 second, then slowly lower the weight back to the starting position. Repeat with the other arm. Only lift the weight once the other arm has returned to the start position.*

Exercises to build powerful shoulders

Superset each exercise with the one below, with only five to ten seconds' rest between sets.

Exercise	Sets and repetitions
Olympic bar shoulder press	3 x 8–12
Arnie shoulder press	3 x 8–12
Upright dumbbell row	3 x 8–12
Upright cable row	3 x 8–12
Single-arm dumbbell frontal raise	3 x 8–12
Cable frontal raise	3 x 8–10

Cable frontal raise

Muscles used Deltoids – middle, anterior, posterior; pectoralis major

1 *Stand with your feet shoulder-width apart, 60cm/2ft from the cable machine. Hold the bar with an overhand grip, with hands just less than shoulder-width apart. Focus on the front of your shoulders. Don't let your back arch.*

2 *Beginning with arms straight down in front of the body, pull the bar up, with your arms straight out in front of you, until it is at eye level. Keep the neck relaxed. Pause for 1 second, then slowly lower it back down to the start position.*

Single-arm cable frontal raise

Muscles used Deltoids – middle, anterior, posterior; pectoralis major

1 *Stand with your feet shoulder-width apart, side-on on to the cable machine. Using one hand, hold the bar with an overhand grip, with the palm facing backward. Stay in a position that is square-on to the machine. Focus on the front of the shoulder that is doing the exercise.*

2 *Keeping your arm straight out in front of you, pull the cable up until it is at eye level. Pause for 1 second, then, without jerking, slowly lower it back down to the start position. Keep the shoulders level and don't let your back arch. Don't hold your breath; keep breathing throughout.*

Bench frontal raise

Muscles used Deltoids – middle, anterior, posterior; pectoralis major; rectus abdominis

1 *Lie face down on a 30-degree incline bench with your arms straight down in front of you just above floor height. Place the balls of your feet on the floor behind you, and out to the sides of the bench. Hold a dumbbell in each hand. Check that the dumbbells are the right weight for you.*

2 *Lift the dumbbells up in front of you with straight arms, keeping the arms as close to each other as possible. Do not allow your lower back to arch. Once your hands are up to almost shoulder level, pause for 1 second, then slowly lower the weights back down to the start position.*

Shoulder Exercises: Stability

The exercises given here use raising movements to place emphasis on the posterior deltoid and middle deltoid muscles – the muscles that provide much-needed stability for a range of movements involved in many sports.

If you want wider, toned shoulders, include the following exercises in your routine. If you have poor posture, use these exercises to prevent rounded shoulders. The exercises will pull your shoulders back and force your back muscles to work in conjunction with your shoulders. They will also help improve your posture. There are many stabilizers in the shoulders, one of which, the scapular (shoulder blade), helps the rotator cuff to stabilize the shoulder joint while in motion. The scapular must be stable – if not, the pressure on it caused by lifting heavy weights may cause injury to the rotator cuff.

These exercises will give you strength with the full range of movement and help to stabilize your shoulder at the same time. Concentrate especially on not using your lower back to help lift the weights. If you are suffering from shoulder injuries, consult your physician before you do these shoulder exercises. While they will help with shoulder stability, your shoulder needs to be sufficiently stable in the first place before you attempt them.

Unless stated otherwise, for each exercise, take 2 to 3 seconds for each direction of the movement. Breathe out at the beginning of the movement, and in as you return to the start position.

Exercises to give wider, toned shoulders	
Exercise	**Sets and repetitions**
Reverse dumbbell shoulder press	3 x 12
Single-arm dumbbell frontal raise	3 x 20
Upright dumbbell row	3 x 12
Bent-over cable lateral raise	3 x 12
Windmill	3 x 12
Single-arm dumbbell lateral raise	3 x 12

Bent-over cable lateral raise

Muscles used Deltoids – middle, anterior, posterior; teres minor; rhomboid; trapezius

1 *Stand between the two arms of the cable machine, with feet just over shoulder-width apart. Take hold of the handle so that your arm is across your body. Bend the upper body at the hips so that your back is parallel to the floor.*

2 *Pull the handle back across your body with a straight arm until it is out to the side, level with your body like the wing of an airplane. Pause for 1 second, then slowly lower the weight back to the start position.*

Bent-over dumbbell lateral raise

Muscles used Deltoids – middle, anterior, posterior; teres minor; rhomboid; trapezius

1 *Sit on the end of a bench with your feet on the floor and legs bent at 90 degrees. Lean forward so that your chest is almost resting on your knees. Hold a dumbbell in each hand.*

2 *Pull the dumbbells out to the sides in an arc, arms almost straight, until the weights are level with the line of your shoulders. Pause for a second, then slowly lower your arms back to the start position.*

Windmill

Muscles used Deltoids – middle, anterior, posterior; rhomboid; trapezius

1 *Stand with your feet shoulder-width apart, arms straight, a dumbbell in each hand in front of you.*

2 *Take your arms out to the side until they are at shoulder level. Pause in this position for 1 second.*

3 *Continue the movement until the weights are above your head. Once they are above your head, slowly lower them back to shoulder level as in step 2, pause for a second, then continue to lower them back to the start position. For this exercise, take 3 to 4 seconds for each direction of the movement.*

Dumbbell lateral raise

Muscles used Deltoids – middle, anterior, posterior

1 *Stand with your feet shoulder-width apart, looking straight ahead, keeping your neck straight. Hold one dumbbell in each hand, with your palms facing toward each other and your elbows tucked in tight against your ribs.*

2 *Keeping your elbows at the same angle, take your arms out to the sides until your upper arm, elbow, forearm and wrist are all level with your shoulders. Pause for a second, then slowly lower back to the start position.*

Single-arm dumbbell lateral raise

Muscles used Deltoids – middle, anterior, posterior

1 *Stand with feet shoulder-width apart, hold a dumbbell in one hand by your side. Let the other hand hang straight and loose by your side to hip level. Tense the core muscles to stop movement and to isolate the deltoid muscle.*

2 *Lift your arm to the side, keeping it straight, until your wrist, forearm and elbow are level with your shoulder. Pause for 1 second, then slowly lower the weight back down to the start position. Repeat with the other arm.*

Biceps Exercises: Powerful Arms

Your biceps make up only 30–40 per cent of your upper arm – the triceps account for most of it – but biceps exercises are probably the most popular upper-body weight-training exercise because, quite simply, many people believe that big biceps look good.

There are two muscle groups in the front of your upper arm. The largest group is the biceps brachii and the smallest is the brachialis. This small area of the body requires a variety of different exercises. It is important to change your bicep routine regularly to get the most from each session. Many gym users use bad technique to lift the heaviest weights they can. The following exercises will ensure that you stick to the correct technique to put the emphasis on your biceps.

For each exercise take 2 to 3 seconds for each direction of the movement. Breathe out at the beginning of the movement, and in as you return to the start position.

Standing barbell bicep curl, wide grip

Muscles used Biceps brachii – long head, short head; brachialis

1 Stand with your feet shoulder-width apart so that you feel well balanced and stable. Grip the barbell close to the thighs, with an underhand grip so that your palms are facing forward, your arms straight and your hands just over shoulder-width apart. To prevent any part of your body other than the biceps from working, keep the upper torso still by tensing your core muscles.

2 Keep your elbows at your sides, locked in to your ribs, and curl the bar up to the shoulders. Prevent your elbows from moving forward and backward: imagine a pin going through your elbow into your ribs; rotate on this axis. Stand side-on to a mirror and glance at it in the middle of each set to check your elbow is in the right place. Pause for 1 second, then slowly return to the start position.

Reverse dumbbell bicep curl

Muscles used Brachioradialis; biceps brachii – long head, short head; brachialis; extensor carpi; radialis – longus, brevis; extensor digitorum; extensor digiti minimi; extensor carpi ulnaris

1 Stand with feet shoulder-width apart. With an overhand grip, hold a dumbbell in each hand, close to your thighs.

2 Keeping your elbows locked in to the ribs, curl the dumbbells up to your shoulders. Pause for 1 second, then slowly return to the start position.

Exercises to build big biceps for beginners		
Exercise	**Sets and repetitions**	**Comments**
Barbell bicep curl	3 x 12	Put these exercises into
Dumbbell bicep curl	3 x 12	pairs and superset them to
Concentration curl	3 x 12	really work your biceps.
Hammer curl	3 x 12	

Standing dumbbell bicep curl

Muscles used Biceps brachii – long head, short head; brachialis

1 *Stand, feet shoulder-width apart, a dumbbell in each hand, close to your thighs, using an underhand grip. To prevent your forearms from overworking, don't grip the dumbbells too tightly.*

2 *Keeping your elbows locked in to your ribs, curl the dumbbells up to your shoulders. Pause for a second, then slowly return to the start position. Keep your palms facing in the same direction. Don't let the weight cof the dumbbell twist them, especially on the way back down.*

Dumbbell hammer curl

Muscles used Brachioradials; biceps brachii – long head, short head; brachialis

1 *Stand with your feet shoulder-width apart, your elbows tucked into your ribs. With an underhand grip, hold one dumbbell in each hand, close to your thighs. Concentrate on the arms doing the work.*

2 *Keep the elbows close to the ribs. Curl the weights up to the shoulders, turning the angle of the forearms by 90 degrees. At the top of the curl, pull the elbows back, pause for a second, then return to the start position.*

Concentration curl

Muscles used Biceps brachii – long head, short head; brachialis

1 *Sitting on a bench, take hold of the dumbbell and rest your elbow against your inner thigh. The palm of your hand should be facing away from you. Try to focus on isolating your bicep.*

2 *Keeping your elbow firmly up against your inner thigh, curl the dumbbell up to your shoulder. Use control to get a good burn. Pause for a second, then lower it down to the start position.*

Biceps Exercises: Strong Lower Arms

Most upper-body exercises will help to work your lower arms but you should also regularly use specific lower-arm exercises. Changing the angle of the wrist when doing biceps curls will make the different parts of the bicep work more effectively.

Forearms need to be strong to give you the support to do other exercises, especially when you need to grip hard and pull weights to work the back muscles.

There are three types of forearm muscle structure and function: forearm supinator, a large muscle on the outer part of the forearm, which can be trained with reverse curls and hammer curls; forearm flexor, a small muscle on the inside of the forearm used to close your fist, which can be trained with barbell wrist curls; and forearm extensors, small muscles on the outside of the forearm, which straighten the fingers after your hand has been clenched, and bring your wrist back toward the arms.

There is virtually no sport which doesn't require strong lower arms. You can adapt your resistance exercises to your chosen sport. If you want stronger arms and wrists for mountain biking do more reps and less sets for greater endurance. Hovering with your fingers over the brakes and hands wrapped around the bars for hour after hour will take its toll if you don't do enough of these exercises. Even if a boxer's lower arms and wrists are heavily wrapped, the muscles must still be able to stand up to the impact and maintain stability to keep throwing punches.

Breathe out when you begin each exercise; then breathe in as you return to the start position.

Exercises to tone and strengthen lower arms	
Exercise	**Sets and repetitions**
Cable bicep curl	3 x 12
Single-arm cable bicep curl	3 x 8
Lying-down cable bicep curl	3 x 12
Wrist curl	3 x 15–20
Reverse wrist curl	3 x 15–20
Hammer wrist curl	3 x 15–20

Cable bicep curl

Muscles used Biceps brachii; brachialis

1 *Stand up straight, arms straight down in front of you, core muscles tense, feet shoulder-width apart, 30cm/1ft from the machine. Grip the bar using an underhand grip, so that the bar rests against the tops of your legs.*

2 *Curl the bar up to the shoulders keeping your elbows tucked into your ribs and your feet shoulder-width apart. Pause for 1 second at the top and then slowly return the bar to the start position.*

Lying-down cable bicep curl

Muscles used Biceps brachii; brachialis

1 *Lie down flat on your back, with your feet close to the cable machine. Hold the bar attached to the cable with an underhand grip, with your hands shoulder-width apart.*

2 *Place the bar down by the front of your legs and curl it up toward your shoulders, keeping your elbows tucked against your ribs. Pause for 1 second then slowly lower it back down.*

Single-arm cable bicep curl

Muscles used Biceps brachii; brachialis

1 *Stand with your feet shoulder-width apart, 30cm/1ft from the cable machine. Grip the bar, with one hand, using an underhand grip, so that it rests against the top of your thigh. Keep your other hand close in by your other thigh. Stand up straight with your core muscles tense. Try to keep the rest of your torso as still as possible.*

2 *Curl the bar up to the shoulder, keeping your elbow tucked in to your ribs. Focus on getting a good full range of movement. Pause for 1 second at the top, then, keeping the core muscles tense, slowly return the bar to the start position. Repeat the same movement on the other side.*

Wrist curl

Muscles used Flexors – carpi ulnaris, digitorum, carpi radialis; palmaris longus

1 *Stand or sit with a barbell in each hand, using an underhand grip, hands shoulder-width apart, elbows at 90 degrees.*

2 *With forearms out in front of you, to isolate the forearm and wrist muscles, curl the weight up as far as possible. Pause for 2 seconds.*

Reverse wrist curl

Muscles used Extensors – carpi radialis longus, carpi radialis brevis, carpi ulnaris, indicis, digitorum

1 *Stand or sit with a dumbbell in one hand, using an overhand grip, elbow bent at 90 degrees to help isolate the forearm and wrist.*

2 *Curl the weight up as far as possible, using just the wrist and forearm muscles, and pause for 2 seconds. Repeat with the other arm.*

Hammer wrist curl

Muscles used Extensors – carpi radialis longus, carpi radialis brevis, carpi ulnaris, digitorum

1 *Stand or sit holding the dumbbell in a hammer position, then gradually allow the weight to tilt your wrist away from you.*

2 *Keep the forearm and arm still and use the muscles in the wrist to tilt the dumbbell back up toward you. Pause for a second then lower to the start position.*

Triceps Exercises

All upper-body resistance training that involves pressing movements will also involve the triceps. If you want to build bigger upper arms or press heavier weights, triceps exercises need to be part of your regular routine.

There are three parts to the triceps muscle: the medial head, lateral head and long head. These muscles are positioned at the back of your upper arm and are responsible for extending your upper arm. Always do your chest or shoulder exercises first before training your triceps. If you have a good session on the triceps, and then try to press weights to work your chest or shoulders, you will not achieve very much. Your triceps will be fatigued long before your chest or shoulders have had a good workout. Compared to the chest or shoulder muscles, the triceps are small muscles, so be strict in your technique to ensure that you are working your triceps only and not other larger muscles.

You need to work hard to get bulging triceps. Remember that roughly 70 per cent of your upper arm mass is made up of the triceps. Once you are strong enough, try to include one or two triceps exercises that involve using your body weight as these are often some of the most effective, and can be of most use to you in everyday life and for your sport.

Remember good technique; if your technique is poor you will be recruiting other muscles such as your chest and shoulders, which will not develop the triceps. For each exercise, take 2 to 3 seconds for each direction of the movement. Breathe out at the beginning of the movement, and breathe in as you return to the start position.

Exercises to build bigger triceps

Exercise	Sets and repetitions
Triceps dip	5 x max
Triceps bench dip	5 x max
Cable push-down	3 x 8–10
Reverse cable push-down	3 x 10
Overhead cable triceps extension	3 x 10

Triceps bench dip

Muscles used Triceps brachii – long head, lateral head, medial head; anconeus

1 *Grip the edge of the bench, with the back of your hands facing forward at your sides, arms fully extended to suspend your body weight. Keep your feet flat on the floor in front of you.*

2 *Lower your body toward the floor, bending your elbows behind you, at 90 degrees. Pause for 1 second, then return to the start position. As you get stronger, take feet farther away from you.*

Triceps dip

Muscles used Triceps brachii – long head, lateral head and medial head; anconeus; pectoralis major

1 *Grip the handles of the machine, with an overhand grip, your legs hanging under you. Keep your elbows tucked in to isolate your triceps. Fully extend your arms to suspend your body weight from the machine.*

2 *Lower your body toward the floor, bending your elbows behind you at 90 degrees. If your elbows are wide apart, you will work the pectorals. Pause for a second, then push yourself back up to the start position.*

Cable push-down

Muscles used Triceps brachii – long head, lateral head and medial head

1 *Use a lighter weight than you think you need to isolate and work the triceps. Grip the bar with an overhand grip, with hands just less than shoulder-width apart, and your arms bent at 90 degrees. Tuck your elbows in against your ribs. Don't let your shoulders rise up.*

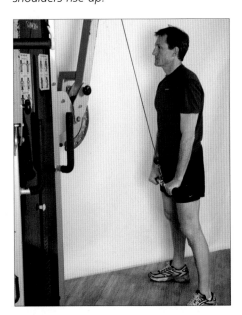

2 *Fully extend your arms, keeping the elbows locked in to your ribs, until your hands are down in front of your legs. Pause for 1 second, then slowly bend your arms, allowing the bar to raise. Open your grip at the bottom of the movement when your arms are in full extension to work your triceps harder.*

Reverse cable push-down

Muscles used Triceps brachii – long head, lateral head and medial head; anconeus; extensors – carpi radialis brevis, digitorum, carpi ulnaris and carpi radialis longus

1 *Grip the bar with an underhand grip, with your hands just less than shoulder-width apart, and arms bent at 90 degrees. Tuck your elbows in closely against your ribs throughout the whole movement.*

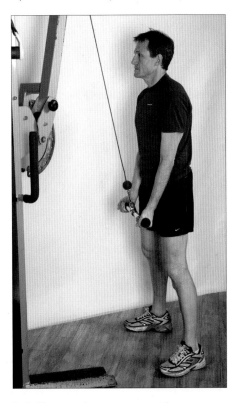

2 *Fully extend your arms until your hands are down in front of your legs. Pause for 1 second, then slowly bend your arms, allowing the bar to raise. Pause for longer at full extension to get a good burn on the triceps.*

Overhead cable triceps extensions

Muscles used Triceps brachii – long head, lateral head and medial head

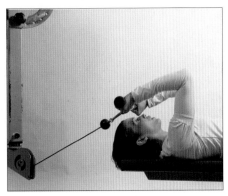

1 *Lie on the bench and grip the bar from behind your head with an overhand grip. Pull it forward so that your arms are bent at 90 degrees and the bar is roughly in line with the front of your head. Your elbows should be facing forward and in a fixed position.*

2 *Bring the bar forward in front of you by fully extending your arms, keeping your elbows as close together as possible. Pause for 1 second on full extension and then bend at the elbow to allow the bar to return to the start position.*

Specific triceps exercises

Many bodybuilders in the past have not used specific triceps exercises and have managed to get away with it because the triceps are involved in so many other exercises, especially chest presses and shoulder presses. Now, however, most bodybuilders do exercises specifically to isolate the triceps and give them that ripped look. The danger is that the triceps can easily be overtrained, especially as they are much smaller than other pressing muscles such as the chest and shoulders. So, avoid making the mistake of thinking that your triceps need to be trained more than your biceps because they make up a bigger percentage of the overall size of your arm when so many exercises work the triceps anyway.

The triceps are a three-headed muscle complex that originates in the shoulder and attaches to the forearm after passing over the top of the elbow. Their function is to straighten your arm from a bent position. They can be worked by moving your arm in an arc in front of you until it is straight down by your side, and also function during pressing movements above the chest or the shoulders.

For really ripped triceps, focus on isolation exercises and spend time on cables, which provide continuous tension throughout the entire movement. It is important to feel the muscle you are isolating, yet many people cheat on triceps exercises by allowing their elbows to move back and forth, making their shoulders and back do the work instead of their triceps. You may need to use a lighter weight than you think you need to achieve proper isolation of the muscle.

For each exercise, take 2 to 3 seconds for each direction of the movement. Breathe out at the beginning of the movement; breathe in as you return to the start position.

Exercises to isolate triceps	
Exercise	**Sets and repetitions**
Triceps press-up	5 x max
Overhead triceps extension	3 x 8–10
Lying-down triceps extension	3 x 8–10
Single-arm cable triceps push-down	3 x 8–10

Single-arm cable triceps push-down

Muscles used Triceps brachii – long head, lateral head and medial head; anconeus

 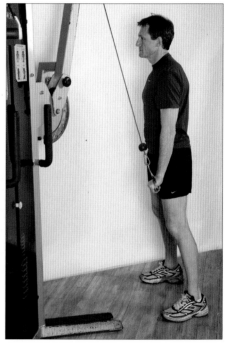

1 Hold the cable handle in one arm using an overhand grip, with your arm bent at 90 degrees and forearms out in front of you. Keep your elbows close to your ribs. Your other arm should rest at your side. Don't let your shoulders rise up in the movement – keep them level and don't let your body twist to help with the movement.

2 Fully extend your arm in a downward direction until your arms are straight and the handle is by your side. Pause for 1 second then slowly allow the arm to bend back up to the starting position at 90 degrees. Hold the full extension for more than 1 second if you want to get even better recruitment of all the tricep muscles.

Triceps press-up

Muscles used Triceps brachii – long head, lateral head and medial head; anconeus

1 Assume the standard press-up position, with hands on the floor, just less than shoulder-width apart, and fingers facing forward. Hold your body up with straight arms. The toes should touch the floor with heels raised.

2 Bend your arms to lower your body, keeping your elbows tucked in close to your ribs. Once the elbows are at 90 degrees pause for 1 second, then press back up extending the arms. This isolates the triceps by using your own body weight.

Overhead triceps extension

Muscles used Triceps brachii – long head, lateral head and medial head

1 *Hold a dumbbell, with an interlocking grip. Slowly take the dumbbell over the top of your head, fully extending your arms. Hold the dumbbell in this position for a few seconds then go on to do step 2. Don't forget to co-ordinate your breathing with the movement and ensure that you are standing in a comfortable position and well balanced.*

2 *Slowly lower the dumbbell behind your head until your arms are bent at 90 degrees. Keep your elbows as close together as possible. Once your elbows go out to the side, you are at the lowest point your flexibility will allow you to go or the weight is too heavy. Pause for 1 second, then push the dumbbell back up above your head by fully extending your arms.*

Lying-down triceps extension

Muscles used Triceps brachii – long head, lateral head and medial head; anconeus

1 *Lie on your back on a flat bench so that your back, shoulders, neck and head are supported. Hold a barbell with an overhand grip, hands no more than shoulder-width apart, up above your shoulders, straight arms, elbows facing forward.*

2 *Keeping your back flat and your feet on the floor, slowly lower the barbell toward your face until your arms are bent at 90 degrees. Pause for 1 second then extend the arm back to the starting position.*

Abdominal Exercises: General

The abdominals are possibly the most important muscles to train in your body. The following exercises, along with the correct techniques to use, provide an effective workout for the full range of abdominal muscles that you need to exercise.

The abdominals, which cover a large area of the mid-section of your body, enable your torso to bend forward and sideways, and to twist. Before you start lifting heavy weights, you need sufficient abdominal training to prevent lower-back injuries. To benefit fully from your training, change the exercises regularly.

These exercises mainly work the rectus abdominis, a large, flat muscle covering the entire front of the abdomen between the lower ribcage and the hips. It contracts to flex your body at the waist and tenses as soon as you start to bring your shoulders and head forward. Sit-ups and leg-raising exercises work the rectus abdominus throughout the entire movement.

For each exercise, take 2 to 3 seconds for each direction of the movement. Breathe out at the beginning of the movement, and breathe in as you return to the start position.

Below: Rectus abdominis, external and internal obliques and the transverse abdominis are the abdominal muscles that support the trunk and hold the organs in place.

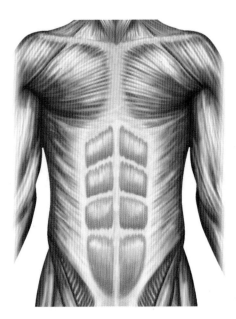

Sit-up

Muscles used Rectus abdominis; obliques – external and internal

1 *Lie on your back and bend your knees to 90 degrees and place your feet flat on the floor. Put your hands behind your head and elbows back out to the sides.*

2 *Tense your abdominals and raise your head, shoulders and upper back off the floor. Pause for 1 second, then lower yourself back down. Keep the abdominals tense throughout.*

Sit-up technique
• Keep your feet on the ground or get your training partner to hold them on the floor. Or, put dumbbells on top of your feet.
• If your neck is weak, tuck your chin in to your chest so it does not move during the exercise.
• Keep your elbows back out to the sides to make the exercise harder.
• You do not need to sit-up – if your abdominals are working, a small movement is enough.

Sit-up with Russian twist

Muscles used Rectus abdominis; obliques – external and internal.

1 *Lie on your back and bend your knees to 90 degrees and place your feet flat on the floor, with your arms up vertically in front of your chest.*

2 *Tense your abdominals and raise your head, shoulders and upper back off the floor. As you sit up, twist your upper body to one side, pause for 1 second, then twist back to straight before slowly returning to the start position. Keep your elbows back out to the sides so that your abdominals will be made to work harder during the movement.*

Exercises to build abdominals for beginners

Exercise	Sets and repetitions
Sit-up	3 x 10
crunch	3 x 10
Sit-up with Russian twist	3 x 10
Reverse crunch with alternate legs bent	3 x 20

Crunch

Muscles used Rectus abdominis; obliques – external and internal

1 *Lie on your back and bend your knees to 90 degrees, lifting the feet off the floor. Put your hands behind your head and your elbows back out to the sides. Tense your abdominals.*

2 *Crunch your knees in and raise your head, shoulders and upper back off the floor. At the top of the crunch pause for 2 seconds, then return to the start position, abdominals still tense.*

Reverse crunch with bent legs

Muscles used Rectus abdominis; external oblique; tensor fascia lata

1 *Lie on your back. Keeping your abdominals tense, pull your legs in toward your abdomen until they are bent at 90 degrees.*

2 *Lower your legs until they are almost parallel to the floor, pause for a second, then return to the start position.*

Reverse crunch with alternate legs bent

Muscles used Rectus abdominis; external oblique; tensor fascia lata

1 *For the starting position, lie on your back and raise your legs, keeping your abdominals tense. Place your hands, palms facing down, flat on the floor, out to your sides in line with your hips.*

2 *Pull one leg in toward your abdomen until the lower part is almost parallel to the floor. Pause for 1 second, then return to the start. Repeat with the other leg. In this way, both sides of your abdominals are working equally.*

Abdominal Exercises: Bodybuilding

For bodybuilders, the abdominals are probably the most important part of their physique. In bodybuilding competitions, judges pay most attention to the contestants' abdominals, looking to see if they are tight, well built and clearly defined.

Great abdominals are a sign of good preparation and dedication to training regularly and appropriately. People often see abdominals as a key indicator of just how fit someone actually is. However, more importantly, abdominals play a crucial role in supporting other working muscles in the body and provide the central support to the back. Many lower-back injuries can be prevented if the abdominals are strong enough to take the stress away from the back. If you do have a back injury, you can reduce back pain through abdominal exercises. Making the abdominal muscles recruit and support your back also massively reduces the work your back has to do.

For each exercise, take 2 to 3 seconds for each direction of the movement. Breathe out at the beginning of the movement, and breathe in as you return to the start position.

Hanging leg raise with twist

Muscles used Rectus – abdominis, femoris; tensor fascia lata; iliopsoas – psoas minor, psoas major and iliacus; obliques – external and internal

1 *Grip a chin-up bar. Hang from the bar, with arms and legs straight to work the abdominals. Tense your abdominals.*

2 *Pull your legs up toward your chest, twisting them to one side to work the abdominals. Pause, then lower them.*

Hanging leg raise

Muscles used Rectus – abdominis, femoris, tensor fascia lata; iliopsoas – psoas minor, psoas major and iliacus

1 *Grip a chin-up bar (any grip). Hang from the bar with your arms and legs straight. Tense your abdominals.*

2 *Crunch your legs up until your thighs are parallel to the floor. Keep your abdominals tensed. Pause for a second, then lower your legs back down.*

Session to build pronounced abdominals	
Exercise	**Sets and repetitions**
Hanging leg raise	3 x 10–20
Crunch	3 x 20–30
Reverse crunch	3 x 20–30
Rope crunch with twist	3 x 20–30
V-crunch	3 x 20–30

Tense abdominals
During both of these hanging leg raises with twist exercises, be aware of how your body moves. It should not swing at any point during the movement. If it does swing, it means that your abdominals are not sufficiently tensed to do their job properly.

Rope crunch

Muscles used Rectus abdominis; external oblique

1 Kneel down, facing the cable machine. Hold the rope and pull it down until it is in front of you at eye height. Lock your arms in this position. Keep the pace of the movement slow so that momentum doesn't take over.

2 Tense your abdominals to keep your back straight and bring the rope down in front of you as far as your abdominals will let you go. Try not to let any part of your body move to help the rope down. Make your abdominals do all the work. Pause for 1 second, then, keeping your abdominals tense, slowly return to the start position.

Rope crunch with twist

Muscles used Rectus abdominis; obliques – external and internal

1 Get down on your knees facing the cable machine. Hold the rope and pull it down until it is in front of you at head height. Lock your arms in this position. Tense your abdominals to keep your back straight.

2 Bring the rope down in front of you as far as your abdominals will let you, twisting to one side to make your oblique muscles do the work. Pause for a second, then slowly return to the start position, abdominals still tense.

V-crunch

Muscles used Rectus abdominis; tensor fascia lata; external oblique

1 Lie on your back with your legs straight up in the air and your feet apart, creating a wide V-shape. With your arms straight, hold your hands together out in front of you, fingers fully extended. You do not need to raise your upper body far off the ground to work your abdominals.

2 Tense your abdominals to bring your head, shoulders and upper back off the floor, pushing your hands between your legs. Keep the crunch slow – don't use your lower back muscles to gather momentum. Pause for 1 second at the top of the crunch, then slowly return to the start position, abdominals still tense.

Abdominal Exercises: The Sides

The following exercises will make you use the sides of your abdominals. To bend to the side and rotate your torso in relation to your hips, you use your oblique muscles, which are made up of the internal obliques, transverse obliques and external obliques.

When you are performing these exercises, stay focused on your abs and be careful to avoid any lateral movement in the hips, because this takes the emphasis away from the abdominal muscles.

If you find it hard to avoid the movement in the hips, try sitting with your legs either side of a bench.

This will prevent your hips moving. Or, you can sit on a fit ball and try to keep the ball as still as possible when you bend to the sides.

For each of these exercises, take 2 to 3 seconds for each direction of the movement. Breathe out at the beginning of the movement, and breathe in as you return to the start position.

Exercises to build side abdominals	
Exercise	**Sets and repetitions**
Side crunch	3 x 20–30
Oblique crunch	3 x 20–30
Dumbbell side bend	3 x 20–30
High cable side bend	3 x 20–30

One-leg crossed crunch

Muscles used Rectus abdominis; external oblique

1 *Lie on your back, with your arms out to the sides, your fingers touching the sides of your head. Cross your left leg over your right leg so that your left ankle rests on your right knee. Keep the movement slow, and focus on the abdominals.*

2 *Tense your abdominals and crunch up toward your knees. At the top of the crunch, twist to one side so that you are facing your left knee. Pause for a second, then slowly lower back down. Repeat the movement with the left leg crossed over the right leg. To put emphasis on the obliques, keep the elbows back and hands relaxed. Look the way you are turning to help the rotation.*

Side crunch

Muscles used Rectus abdominis; obliques – external and internal

1 *Lie on your right side, with your legs slightly bent, your left hand behind your head, and your right arm tucked across your body. Stay as side-on as possible to make the crunch more effective.*

2 *Tense your abdominals, keep your feet firmly together and crunch up sideways as far as you can go. Keep your left hand slightly behind your head and your right arm tucked across your body throughout. Turn over and repeat the movement with the opposite side. As long as the obliques are working, the range of movement can be small to begin with.*

Dumbbell side bend

Muscles used Rectus abdominis; obliques – external and internal

1 *Stand with your legs shoulder-width apart and your right hand behind your head. Hold a dumbbell in your left hand, down at your side.*

2 *Keeping your abdominals tense and staying side-on, bend at the hips to lower down to the side that holds the dumbbell. Once the dumbbell is level with your knee, pause for 1 second, then raise your body back up to the start position. Repeat with the other side. As you stretch down, you will be lengthening your abdominals, and on the way back up, you will be contracting them to make them work harder.*

High cable side bend

Muscles used Rectus abdominis; obliques – external and internal

1 *Stand side-on to the cable machine, feet shoulder-width apart. Take hold of the pulley with one hand and hold it at shoulder height, with your arm bent. Let your other hand hang by your side. Keep the arm holding the cable as still as possible to ensure that it is only the abdominals that are doing the work.*

2 *Tense your abdominals and crunch down to the side. Try holding the position at the bottom of the bend for longer to really isolate the correct muscles. Pause at the bottom for 1 second, then slowly come back up to the start position. Repeat the movement on the other side.*

Oblique crunch

Muscles used Rectus abdominis; obliques – external and internal

1 *Lie on your back with your legs bent and over to the left side, your feet placed firmly together. Try to keep your shoulders on the floor and your legs as far over to one side as possible. Place your hands behind your head with your elbows out to the side, with your fingers, fully extended, touching the sides of your head.*

2 *Tense your abdominals and crunch up, keeping your upper body as square-on as possible. Pause for a second at the top of the crunch and then, keeping your abdominals tense, slowly return to the start position. To make the abdominals work harder, tense them equally on the way back to the start as you did on the way up. Repeat on the other side.*

Abdominal Exercises: Rotational

It is important to use abdominal exercises that simulate the types of movements you need to do in everyday life and for your sport. The following exercises involve rotational exercises. Virtually every sporting activity calls for good rotational strength.

You should always maintain your abdominal muscles in tension throughout any exercise. If you can practise this in your strength workouts, you will start to use these muscles without having to make any conscious effort to do so. Get in touch with your abdominal muscles mentally – you need to learn how to recruit them and how to isolate the different abdominal muscles with various exercises.

When you train your abdominals, you should feel a burn and as you train harder, the burn should intensify. As your abdominal muscles get stronger, you will feel the burn even more as they work that bit harder. Your abdominals should feel pumped up after a workout, just like any other body part you have been training.

Be careful not to attempt too many repetitions. If your abdominal muscles get tired, you will start to use your lower back, which can lead to back injuries and overdevelopment of the lower-back muscles. To avoid using your lower back, always keep your abdominals tensed as you return to the start position in any abdominal exercise. The negative phase of the movement can make a massive difference in your abdominal development.

For each of these exercises, take 2 to 3 seconds for each direction of the movement. Breathe out at the beginning of the movement; breathe in as you return to the start position.

Excercises to tone and build rotational strength	
Exercise	**Sets and repetitions**
Hanging leg raise with a twist	3 x 10–20
Broomstick twist	3 x 30–40
Kneeling cable rotation	3 x 30–40
Alternating leg crunch	3 x 20–30

Alternating leg crunch

Muscles used Rectus abdominis; obliques – external and internal; tensor fascia lata; quadriceps

1 *Lie on your back, with your arms out to the sides, your fingers touching the sides of your head. Raise both legs up in the air at 90 degrees so that your calves are parallel to the floor. Keep your feet firmly together. Ensure that the movement is slow and under control to make your abdominals do all the work.*

2 *Straighten your right leg and crunch up with a twist, bringing your right elbow toward your left knee. When your elbow touches your knee, pause for 2 seconds, then return to the start position. Repeat with the other side. To make this exercise harder, try performing it on a slight incline.*

Leg criss-cross

Muscles used Rectus abdominis; obliques – external and internal; tensor fascia lata; quadriceps

1 *Lie on your back with your legs on the floor stretched straight out in front of you. Put your hands by your sides, with your palms flat on the floor, for added stability. Press your back flat against the floor throughout the movement.*

2 *Lift your legs into the air and criss-cross them, alternating right over left and left over right. Keep your hands by your sides. To check that your lower abdominals are working, put your fingers under your lower back. You will feel it pushing against your fingers.*

Kneeling cable rotation

Muscles used Rectus abdominis; obliques – external and internal

1 *Kneel on the floor, side-on to one side of the cable machine. Keeping your arms straight and together in a V shape and your lower body straight from the abdomen down, grip the handle firmly with both hands.*

2 *Tense your abdominals and rotate at the waist, taking your arms from one side to the other in a semicircular movement. When you have rotated through 180 degrees, pause for 1 second, then return – again through a semicircular movement – to the start position.*

Machine trunk rotation

Muscles used Rectus abdominis; obliques – external and internal

1 *Sit on the machine and wrap your arms around the supports to keep yourself facing forward. Emphasize the abdominals throughout the movement.*

2 *Tense your core muscles and rotate from one side to the other, keeping the movement smooth. Try not to move the hips and shoulders too much.*

Broomstick twist

Muscles used Rectus abdominis; obliques – external and internal

1 *Stand with your feet shoulder-width apart so that you feel well balanced. Hold a broomstick or similar lightweight pole behind your head, across the back of your shoulders.*

2 *Keeping your feet firmly shoulder-width apart, rotate your upper body from one side to the other, keeping your hips as still as possible so that you can put more emphasis on the obliques.*

NUTRITION

To get the most from your fitness training, you need to focus on nutrition as much as exercise. No matter how hard you train, if you eat the wrong food at the wrong time, you will hinder your progress and may also experience fatigue, illness and injury. This chapter reveals the reality behind quick-fix diets and explains why you should simply eat healthily. The key is to know which foods are good for you, when to eat them and their effect on your performance. Equipped with this knowledge you can adopt a healthy eating plan to suit your lifestyle and help achieve your exercise goals.

Above: Include a selection of green vegetables in your diet to get vitamins and minerals.
Left: One of your portions of five-a-day could be a fresh fruit juice.

Eating Healthily

With so much conflicting advice on how to eat healthily, it can be difficult knowing which foods are best and the correct time to eat them, especially when you are exercising hard. But it doesn't have to be such a problem.

A regular exercise routine throws up many questions about diet. Should you eat a diet rich in carbohydrates or go for the high protein option? Should you have separate protein days and carbohydrate days? Should you focus on eating foods labelled low fat? Is it best to have three meals a day or several smaller meals? If you are exercising hard, what and when should you eat? Which diet will work for you?

Diet confusion

Before changing your eating habits, consider what our ancestors ate 10,000 years ago. After all, the human body has not changed in all that time, and neither have our dietary requirements. We are designed to be hunter-gatherers, not to live sedentary lifestyles, consuming convenience foods rich in sugar, saturated fats and salt. Despite the lack of healthcare, our ancestors had relatively good health – chronic diseases, such as obesity, diabetes, liver disease and heart disease were far less prevalent than they are today. There are still areas of the world where people live as our ancestors did 10,000 years ago.

Below: Apples and carrots make a great, low-calorie snack when you are hungry. And they are full of vitamins and fibre.

Above: Fruits tend to be low in calories and fat and provide fibre and vitamins as well as natural sugars.

These people do not suffer from high cholesterol, high blood pressure and insulin problems. Instead, they have a low percentage of body fat and very efficient cardiovascular systems.

A natural diet

Hunter-gatherers had to think of food as fuel. They ate what they were naturally meant to eat. In the modern developed

Below: Don't rely on fast food; take your own healthy lunch of nuts, seeds, dried fruit and canned fish.

Above: Fish, such as smoked salmon with scrambled eggs, makes a tasty and delicious start to the day.

world, people choose foods that satisfy their tastebuds without considering how it will affect their daily performance, whether it's running for the bus or concentrating in the office. Far too many modern-day city dwellers do not eat a natural diet, as dictated by our genes. Instead, the supermarkets tell us what we should eat, even though 75 per cent of the food available in those packed aisles would not have been available 200 years ago. For example, adverts extol the virtues of cereal as a breakfast food, but cereals were only introduced at the time of the agricultural revolution.

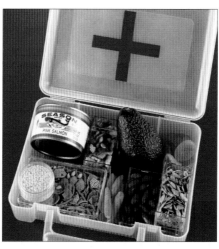

Slowly does it
Don't alter your eating habits all at once; it is important to remember that you should make any changes to your diet gradually so that your body can adjust and get used to the healthier foods. Don't expect to see spectacular results such as weight loss overnight. The first thing you should notice, though, if you are making the right changes to your diet is an increase in your energy levels.

Above: Fresh vegetables supply vitamins and minerals. It is important to eat a good variety to get vitamins A and C.

Many types of cereals are of little nutritional value. Eating fresh fish and fruit for the first meal of the day is a much healthier option than a bowl of cornflakes.

What's on your plate?

Because we are not eating a diet to which we are naturally suited, we are suffering from a wide range of health problems. Just as you need to use the correct fuel in your car, your body needs the correct food to function properly, and to avoid being damaged. So, take time to study foods and find out where the food you eat comes from. Are the meats, fruit and vegetables on your plate organically or agrochemically produced? Wherever possible, it is better to eat organic food for a number of reasons:

• Organic foods contain higher levels of essential vitamins and minerals.
• It tastes better, especially fruit and vegetables, which take a longer

time to grow and contain a lower proportion of water than the equivalent agrochemical produce.
• Only 32 of the 290 food additives used in food production are used in organic food. Many food additives have been linked with health problems.
• Organic foods have not been genetically modified.
• There are no drugs in organic foods.
• Organic foods contain none of the many chemicals used to make agrochemical foods grow faster.
• Producers of organic foods undergo regular inspection to ensure high standards are maintained.
• Organic food production does not contribute to the pollution and degradation of the environment.
• Animal welfare is a priority for organic producers. Animals reared humanely and fed the appropriate diet in free-range environments means better, more nutritious food – which, in turn, means a healthier you.

The bonfire theory

Your body's metabolism works in exactly the same way as a bonfire. But which type? Essentially, there are two types to choose from:

The log bonfire is fed with logs every two to three hours. It takes time to light this fire, but once lit, it burns with intense heat for a long time.

The twig bonfire is easy to light, but soon goes out and emits very little heat.

Eat little and often

If you leave a gap of more than three to four hours between eating, your metabolism will slow down, just like the bonfire that goes out if it is not fed every two to three hours.

If you fuel your body with foods high in sugar, your metabolism will be very sluggish and your body will only be able to perform when you keep taking more sugar. In this scenario, your metabolism is just like the twig bonfire. Your body never burns fat because it is constantly being provided with top-ups of sugar to keep it going.

However, fuelling your body with the correct fats, proteins and natural, slow-releasing carbohydrates will keep your metabolism high and enable your body to use fat as a good energy source – just like the log bonfire. If you can follow this theory for most of your everyday meals, you will be on the way to becoming a healthier person, and you will soon experience an increase in energy levels and improved body shape.

Below: The bonfire analogy is that, fed with nourishing food every few hours, the body will keep going for a long time.

Quality not quantity

You should concentrate on the type of calories that you eat and timing when you eat, rather than focus on the number of calories consumed.

Fluid Intake

Your body is 70 per cent water and you should do your best to keep it that way during exercise, so fluid intake is vital. Fluid loss will depend on the intensity of your exercise, the duration, temperature, humidity and your fitness level.

Muscles produce heat, which makes you sweat. This, in turn, provides a layer of moisture on the skin that helps to keep the core temperature down. Your body's temperature has to remain between 37°C/98.6°F and 38°C/100.4°F for it to function properly. For every 1 litre/ 2 pints of sweat that evaporates, you lose 600kcal of heat energy. A depletion of body fluids is called dehydration.

Below: Dehydration is one of the main causes for poor sporting performance. Your body is 70 per cent water and needs hydration during sporting activities.

It is important to know how to avoid becoming dehydrated, and to recognize the symptoms if you become dehydrated. One simple test is to weigh yourself before and after exercise. Typically, you will lose 1 litre/2 pints of fluid per hour and around 2 litres/4 pints per hour when the temperature and humidity are high.

A 2 per cent weight loss will mean a 20 per cent decrease in performance; lose 4 per cent and you may have nausea, vomiting and diarrhoea; 5 per cent and your brain will start to shut down; 7 per cent and you hallucinate; 10 per cent and heatstroke sets in.

Above: Always carry water with you so you can keep well hydrated at all times in training at the gym.

Exercise and hydration

To avoid dehydration, drink plenty of fluids before, during and after exercise. Drink 400–600ml/13–20fl oz of fluid in the two hours before exercise. It may be fairly easy to drink on a bike, but it is much harder to drink during activities such as running, so make sure that you have plenty of fluid in your system before you start exercising. It is not possible to take in extra fluid and store it. Above a certain level, your body will pass it as urine. Include some carbohydrates in a drink, such as simple sugars: 1g/0.04oz of carbohydrate for every 1kg/2.2lb of body weight, or 14g/0.5oz per 18kg/40lb will help to sustain energy levels.

To maintain the exercise intensity level during exercise, you must replace 80 per cent of your fluid loss during exercise.

Dehydration test

Check the colour of your urine – the darker the urine, the more dehydrated you have become.

Above: Staying hydrated means you will need to calculate how much fluid to drink, how often and what your fluids should contain.

Try to drink before you feel thirsty. Aim to drink 400–1,000ml/13–34fl oz per hour. If you leave it too long, you may end up feeling sick and bloated. Drink plain water if exercise lasts up to 1 hour. For longer exercise sessions, use sports drinks that contain hypotonic or isotonic solutions, which will help with water absorption; and glucose polymers, which will allow you to absorb a greater quantity of carbohydrate to keep your energy levels high.

The following is a guide to which drinks are best according to the exercise you are doing:
• Isotonic: Use for middle- or long-distance running events and team sports. It provides glucose, the body's preferred source of energy. For a concentration of 6–10 per cent, for example, try Lucozade Sport, 515g/18oz, and High Five; or mix 200ml/6.7fl oz orange squash, 1 litre/2 pints water and 1g/0.04oz salt.
• Hypotonic: Use for car racing and horse-racing. It quickly replaces fluid loss but contains no carbohydrate; mix 100ml/3.4fl oz orange squash, 1 litre/2 pints water and 1g/0.04oz salt.
• Hypertonic: Use to top up carbohydrate during long-distance events. It is suitable when energy is required for long periods, can be taken on the move and is easy to digest; mix 400ml/13.5fl oz orange squash, 1 litre/2 pints water and 1g/0.04oz salt.

After exercise To enable a fast, efficient recovery, slowly drink 1.5 litres/3 pints of fluid for every 1kg/2.2lb of weight loss. Between exercise sessions, drink 1 litre/2 pints for every 1,000kcal of energy expenditure.

Overhydration

It is possible to overhydrate if you drink too much. This leads to circulatory problems and dizziness as the blood becomes too diluted, or even seizures or coma if overhydration occurs quickly. If you suspect that you are overhydrated, stop drinking and consume something salty, as your sodium levels will probably have become dangerously low.

Caffeine

Your performance can be improved by caffeine; it helps your body to use fatty acids instead of glycogen, which will enable you to exercise at a high intensity for longer. But more than 300mg of caffeine can be detrimental to your health, as it may cause dehydration (a cup of coffee typically contains 50–100mg of caffeine). Increase your water intake to counteract the dehydrating effect of caffeine.

Alcohol

There are very few benefits to drinking alcohol. It may be useful in social situations – even then, in moderation only – but beyond that, there's little to recommend it. It will affect your reaction time and co-ordination, and you will experience a decline in your speed, power and strength. It will hinder your body's ability to regulate temperature and can lead to blood-sugar level problems and dehydration. The empty calories in alcohol will also lead to weight gain. If you do choose to drink alcohol, make sure that you also drink plenty of water to dilute its effects and reduce the risk of dehydration.

Below: Drinking tea and coffee will make you even more dehydrated. It is best to stick to water or juice.

Below: Lack of fluid can make you prone to headaches, lower your energy levels and make you feel unwell.

Eating to Lose Weight

Fad diets are everywhere and promise miraculous results. In truth, however, beyond healthy book sales and magazine circulation figures, they do little good. Long-term weight loss involves a realistic plan that encompasses lifestyle, diet and exercise.

No single diet, whether it is low fat, reduced calorie or low carbohydrate, will help you to maintain your new size once you have lost the initial weight. One of the first things all of these diets do is lower your normal calorie intake. This will cause you to lose weight, but much of this weight loss will be muscle, which you need to retain, because it is living tissue that helps you to maintain a high metabolism and keep you trim. If you want to lose weight, and keep it off, you need to change your lifestyle and eating habits. Another important factor is to understand the relationship between what you eat and what you look like. Also regular exercise will help you in your goal.

Here are 16 steps that will help you to lose weight:

1 Portion control This is one of the fastest ways to lose weight. If you use a smaller plate, and don't pile food up, you will soon find that your stomach starts to shrink and that you feel full

Below: When you are trying to lose weight, choose ingredients for your meal that are fresh and healthy.

after eating less food. Aim to eat 80 per cent of what you think you need at each meal.

2 Eat slowly Chew each mouthful at least 20 times before you swallow it. Taking longer to eat your food will send a signal to your brain to register that your stomach is full. While you are chewing, put your knife and fork down to create a slight pause between mouthfuls. Again, this will enable you to feel full before you have time to have a second plateful.

3 Leave leftovers Only eat the food on your plate if you really need it. There is no shame in not finishing a meal, especially if you are out in a restaurant and you have been presented with a larger portion than you wanted.

4 Less fat Eat less fatty food. In particular, avoid eating fat from foods that have been processed. Also, cook with less fat to avoid adding extra fat to your meal.

5 More fruit and vegetables A low-calorie way to feel full is to eat lots of fruit and vegetables. Eating more of these foods will also help to increase the fibre in your diet, which will help

Above: Don't feel you always have to finish everything on your plate – stop eating when you are satisfied.

to lower your cholesterol level. Aim for at least five portions of fruit and vegetables each day.

6 Read the label Be wary of foods that are labelled 'low fat'. They may be low in saturated fats but the likelihood is that they are high in sugar, which will

Below: Eat foods that are not processed and are as natural as possible so you know what is in them.

Above: Above: If you need to lose weight, select low-fat foods, such as fruits and vegetables, and control the portion size.

Above: If you are trying to lose weight, and you eat in a restaurant, ask about the ingredients and how the food is cooked so you can make the right choice.

have the effect of raising your blood sugar, then your insulin levels and make you deposit fat.

7 Low GI Eat low GI foods to prevent your body becoming insulin-resistant (a pre-diabetic state in which normal amounts of insulin are no longer sufficient to produce a normal insulin response from fat, muscle and liver cells). Eating low GI foods will keep your blood-sugar levels constant and enable you to feel good and crave healthy foods.

8 Be prepared When travelling, take with you food such as nuts and fruits, so that you don't have to rely on what is on offer at the service station or garage and be tempted to buy chocolate.

9 Little and often Eat small meals regularly to make sure that your metabolism is working all the time. Don't let yourself go hungry, because your body will then go into 'famine mode' and start to store all the calories, thinking it won't be fed again for a while.

10 Drink more water You might often think that you are hungry when, in fact, you are just thirsty. Avoid excessive calories from other beverages such as fizzy drinks and alcohol. Aim for eight 200ml/6.7-fl oz glasses per day.

11 Avoid sugary snacks You may think that just one sugary snack a day won't do much harm when you count the small number of calories in it. However, the knock-on effect on your energy levels, and the associated problems with insulin levels, should not be underestimated.

12 Ask about what you are eating If you are eating out, find out what the ingredients of a dish are, and don't be embarrassed to ask the chef to omit a sauce, dressing or gravy, if necessary.

13 Get active No matter how healthily you eat, if you don't do any activity, you will not be able to burn off calories. You need to be burning off more calories in a day than you consume in order to lose weight.

14 Slowly does it Don't rush it – aim to lose weight at a sensible speed. A loss of 0.5–1kg/1.1–2.2lb per week is sustainable, and will give your body a chance to adjust to the changes it is going through.

15 Obstacles Note down anything that gets in the way of losing weight, then work out ways that you can get around these obstacles.

16 Downfalls List the foods that made you put on weight in the first place. You need to understand which foods are bad for you in order to make yourself avoid them altogether by not buying them or, at least, cut down on the amount you eat.

Below: Sugary snacks such as chocolate will be detrimental to weight loss; instead, opt for fruit or nuts.

Eating to Gain Muscle

Some people think that hour after hour at the gym is all they need to build muscle. You can train all day long, but if you don't put the right fuel into your body, your muscles will fail to recover after exercising and simply will not grow.

To gain muscle, you need to adopt a diet that is rich in carbohydrate and protein, with some fat. Choose low GI foods over high GI ones and consider including a dietary supplement.

Small and frequent meals will help to increase metabolism, burn more fat and give you better muscle definition – great definition will make your muscles look bigger, even if they aren't. Eat little and often; every three to four hours to avoid going into a catabolic state, in which your body starts to eat muscle to get energy, resulting in more fat and less muscle.

A balanced diet

Each meal should consist of 40 per cent carbohydrate, 40 per cent protein and 20 per cent fat. You need protein to build muscle and carbohydrates to give you the energy to turn protein into muscle. Fats are also important, as every cell in the body has fat in it and hormones are made from fats. Choose unsaturated fats – good sources are fish oils, peanut butter and olive oil.

Testosterone is the most important hormone as far as muscle growth is concerned. A low-fat diet leads to low

Above: Putting in a sustained effort at each session in the gym will pay off over time as you get fitter.

Left: Protein, such as a lean steak, is an essential nutrient for repairing and building muscles.

Measure fat
You should aim to gain around 250g/0.5lb of muscle per week. If you gain any more than that, you will be in danger of putting on fat instead of muscle. In addition to using the scales, measure your body fat on a regular basis.

levels of testosterone, and therefore no muscle growth. Every tissue in the body is made from protein, so it is very important to maintain a high-protein diet, especially if you need to repair damaged tissue after exercise.

Protein levels

For basic training of up to an hour a day, you need to consume 2.5g/0.08oz of protein per 1kg/2.2lb of body weight. If you aim to train hard and gain muscle, you will need to increase this to 3–4g/0.10–0.14oz of protein per 1kg/2lb of body weight, or approximately 57–85g/2–3oz per 18kg/40lb.

There is no point in eating more than 4g/0.14oz of protein per 1kg/2.2lb of body weight, or approximately 3oz per 40lb, as your body cannot utilize more than this quantity of protein.

Low GI and high fibre

Eat low GI foods for a sustained slow, but constant release of energy, and to maximize recovery of your muscles. Always include fibre in your diet. Five to ten servings of fruit and vegetables a day will help to keep your digestive system working efficiently, which is especially important if you are eating extra protein. Fibre will slow down the digestion of the protein giving your body more time to absorb the amino acids.

Below: Peanut butter provides essential fats and protein for building muscles and a long steady release of energy.

Above: Avoid saturated fats; choose healthy oils instead, such as olive oil or various types of nut oils.

Food supplements

Creatine supplementation will help to increase muscle mass. It is possible to gain up to 3 per cent muscle mass in one week, if you consume 7g/0.25oz of creatine a day. Creatine works by dragging water into the cells, which then stimulate protein synthesis.

There are some side effects – water retention, cramping, kidney and muscle damage and dehydration. The best form of creatine is creatine monohydrate, which is readily available and easy for the body to utilize.

People with fewer fast-twitch muscle fibres may struggle to get the maximum benefit from taking creatine. If you are a long-distance athlete looking to put on weight, use creatine after meals containing carbohydrates, as the increase in the insulin level after the meal can help with the uptake of creatine into the muscle cells. Drink plenty of water after taking creatine to compensate for its dehydrating effect.

Meal-replacement drinks If you lead a busy lifestyle, it can be hard to prepare meals with enough calories and nutritional value. A meal-replacement drink (MRP) will take care of that. Most MRP drinks contain essential amino acids and creatine

Calorie count

If you are attempting to put on muscle, try increasing your carbohydrate consumption to 50 per cent and your fat consumption to 25 per cent, while decreasing your protein consumption to 25 per cent. This will mean that instead of consuming 12 calories per 500g/1.1lb of body weight, which is an average amount, you will double your calories and consume 24 calories per 500g/1.1lb of body weight. Extra calories are essential if you want to put on more muscle, especially if you are burning off more energy because you have recently stepped up your physical training.

and glutamine to aid recovery and promote muscle growth. They typically contain 40g/1.4oz of protein and 60g/2oz of carbohydrates.

Exercise and rest

To prevent calories from being burnt, avoid cardiovascular exercise and ensure you do appropriate weight-training. Use free weights to work throughout the entire movement and provide good stability. Rest is very important. If your body has maximum recovery after a workout, it will also have maximum potential for growth.

Below: Adding protein and fruit shakes to your diet will ensure that you get a supply of high-quality protein.

Eating for Endurance

For an endurance event, such as a marathon, you need to maximize the amount of fuel your body can store, take on more during the event and quickly replenish yourself after the race for a speedy recovery.

In the two or more days before an endurance event or long training session, start to prepare your body. You should top up your muscle glycogen levels by regularly eating plenty of low GI foods.

To make sure your muscles are fully hydrated, make sure that you consume 30 per cent more fluids than normal in the three to four days prior to the event. Avoid drinking any alcohol and do not eat foods that are high in fat. If you get nervous before a big event, avoid eating too much fibre, as this can upset your stomach. Also, avoid any foods with which you are not familiar. Eat five to six smaller meals throughout the day, with no more than four hours between each meal.

Below: Before the big event, when you are training, eat what you will have on race day so that you know your body is comfortable with it.

Carb loading

Although it does not work for everyone, carbohydrate loading is popular among endurance athletes. It involves lowering your carbohydrate intake to 5–7g/ 0.2–0.3oz per 1kg/2.2lb of body weight, or approximately 113–170g/4–6oz per 18kg/40lb for three days; then raising it to 8–10g/0.3–0.4oz per 1kg/2.2lb of body weight, or about 170–227g/6–8oz per 18kg/40lb, for the final three days before the event.

Try this technique in preparation for a long training session to see if it works for you before adopting it for an event.

One day before the event

At this stage you need to continue topping up your muscle glycogen levels (stored glucose, mainly in the liver and the muscles) by eating low GI foods, avoiding fatty foods, alcohol and too much fibre. Eat simple, familiar foods that you find easy to digest. If you are

Endurance length

Endurance events refer to those events lasting for more than 90 minutes, including marathons, half-marathons, cycle races and triathlons.

staying away from home and having food prepared for you, check the ingredients for anything that could upset your digestion and hydration levels. Take particular note of the salt and spice content.

The day of the event

Eat your main meal two to four hours before the start. You may need to experiment with this in training. Some people need at least three hours after eating before exercise, while others need only two hours. Consume foods that are low in fat, protein and fibre. The meal should consist of 2.5g/0.08oz of carbohydrate

Above: Plan your food intake during an event such as a marathon so that you do not run out of energy too early in the race.

per 1kg/2.2lb of body weight, or approximately 42.5g/1.5oz per 18kg/40lb.

Sometimes, having food in the form of a carbohydrate drink is a better way to aid digestion, especially if you suffer from a nervous digestion system. The carbohydrates can be a mixture of low and high GI. The high GI foods will give you the initial boost that you need, while the low GI foods will release energy steadily over the course of the event.

During the event

You could be using more than 1,000 calories per hour during an endurance event. As you can only store 2,000 calories before you start exercise, and only then if you have maximized your nutrition, it is essential to eat as you compete. Aim to take on 400–600 calories per hour, eating every 15–20 minutes. The foods should consist of 70 per cent carbohydrate, 20 per cent fat

and 10 per cent protein. Consume foods such as energy bars, gels, bananas, dried fruit, cereal bars and low GI energy drinks that contain little fibre and are easy to digest. If the event lasts for more than four hours, you will need to

Below: Take on fluid containing essential minerals, which will help you to sustain energy in your muscles.

use fat as an energy source. Therefore, you will need to have consumed adequate amounts of carbohydrate, because your body cannot utilize fat without it.

Drink 200ml/6.7fl oz of water for every 100 calories consumed to prevent water being taken from the muscles and transferred to the gut to digest the food, which will have a detrimental effect on your performance. Drinks containing electrolytes will help to replace essential minerals such as sodium, chloride, calcium, potassium and magnesium.

After the event

After exercise, your body is ready to take in and store carbohydrates better than at any other time. In the 30–45 minutes after exercise, you will be able to process carbohydrates up to three times faster than at any other time of the day, so take advantage of this fact. Consume a mixture of low and high GI foods to replenish glycogen stores quickly and prepare for the next workout. Try taking food in the form of liquid to make it easier to digest. The ratio of carbohydrate to protein after exercise should be in the region of 4:1.

Below: As soon as possible after the event, make sure you replace all the fluid that you have lost.

Index